Achieving

QTS

meeting the **professional standards framework**

Teaching
Religious
Education

Primary and Early Years

Achieving

QTS

meeting the **professional standards framework**

Teaching Religious Education

Primary and Early Years

Elaine McCreery, Sandra Palmer and Veronica Voiels

LearningMatters

First published in 2008 by Learning Matters Ltd.

British Library Cataloguing in Publication Data
A CIP record for this book is available from the British Library.

ISBN: 978 1 84445 108 1

Cover design by Topics
Text design by Code 5 Design Associates Ltd
Project management by Deer Park Productions, Tavistock
Typeset by PDQ Typesetting Ltd, Newcastle under Lyme
Printed and bound in Great Britain by Bell & Bain Ltd, Glasgow

Learning Matters
33 Southernhay East
Exeter EX1 1NX
Tel: 01392 215560
info@learningmatters.co.uk
www.learningmatters.co.uk

Contents

Preface

This book brings together the philosophy, ideas and experience of three teachers of religious education (RE). Between us we have taught thousands of trainee teachers over 30 years and have followed and been part of the development of RE taught in schools.

Our aim is to continue to advance and support the teaching and development of RE in primary schools. Underpinning this aim is a central belief in the importance and value of RE for young people. At its heart, RE is about the eternal human desire to understand and relate to life in all its facets. RE involves children in examining and exploring those matters that are of primary concern to humankind: *RE provokes challenging questions about the ultimate meaning and purpose of life* (Religious Education: The Non-Statutory National Framework, QCA, 2004, p18). RE also offers children the opportunity to reflect on their own beliefs and experiences and those of others in order to help them understand their relationship to the rest of the world. For many children this will also involve them in reflecting on their relationship with God.

Sometimes there has been uncertainty about RE and a lack of clarity about its purpose – especially in a multifaith society such as Britain. This book therefore seeks to clarify misunderstandings and offer practical approaches to developing effective, meaningful RE in primary classrooms.

This book is written primarily for you as a trainee teacher, providing an introduction to the subject as part of your familiarisation with the primary curriculum. However, it can also be used by practising teachers, who will be able to use it for developing their own RE teaching. Parents and school governors could use it to help them understand what their children are doing in RE. Finally, teacher trainers could use it to support their teaching of RE on QTS courses.

The book has been structured to give you a thorough overview of the principles of good RE which then culminate in the planning process. However, each chapter can be read on its own if particular aspects of RE are of interest. Throughout the book you will also find tasks that can be used on your own or in a group to help you think about some of the issues that are raised in each chapter. The Appendix gives you an introduction to the six major world religions and how they fit geographically and historically.

By the end of the book, you will have a fuller understanding of the place of RE in the primary curriculum and the value it has for helping children to learn more about themselves and the world in which they live.

E. McCreery
S. Palmer
V. Voiels
2008

1
RE in England and Wales: the law, the curriculum and attainment targets

Chapter objectives

By the end of this chapter you will have developed knowledge and understanding of:

- **the law regarding RE;**
- **the role of a Standing Advisory Council for Religious Education;**
- **the location of the curriculum for RE;**
- **the aims and objectives of RE;**
- **the Attainment Targets for RE;**
- **RE and school worship.**

This chapter addresses the following Standards for QTS: **Q3a**

Introduction

Religious education (RE) can be one of the most dynamic and exciting areas of the curriculum to teach, for it is here that children can gain an understanding of the rich world of faith and explore some of those questions which are fundamental to human existence. Who am I? What is the purpose to life? What are my responsibilities to others? What will happen after death? How should I react to someone whose beliefs are different from mine? These are just some of the questions of meaning and purpose which form the core of RE as it is conceived in the law of England and Wales. These questions are not explored in a vacuum but in learning about beliefs and practices of different religions.

The notion that you should explore such big questions with young children and help them understand the world of religion may feel quite daunting. This book is written to help you. However, before you can begin to think about how to teach the subject you need to understand what the subject is about.

REFLECTIVE TASK

Before you start to read the rest of the chapter stop and think about your own religious education. What did you do? What do you think was the point of it?

How do you feel about it? Write your answers down so that you can return to them at the end of the chapter.

The law: what you need to know

Each country has its own understanding of RE. In Australia, for example, children are taught a social studies syllabus in which children learn about religion in society but also have a period of religious instruction given by teachers, usually volunteers, from their own Christian denomination or another faith. In France and the U S A the teaching of religion is banned in state schools. In Germany children receive denominational teaching.

A particular understanding of RE has evolved in the British context though, as in any subject, there are debates and controversies. This understanding of RE is embodied in the law as expressed in statutes and guidance. It is important that you have a good grasp of the legal requirements and understand its implications for you as a professional: *Be aware of the professional duties of teachers and the statutory framework within which they work* (Q3a).

The types of legal documentation

- Acts of Parliament and statutory circulars regarding the content of RE. Local authorities are bound to obey these documents.
- Non-statutory guidance about the content of RE. It is here that we find guidance about the aims and objectives of RE. These documents are offered as guidance to the implementation of the law.
- Local Agreed Syllabuses for RE (see below).
- Diocesan syllabuses or those supplied by the religious foundation of the school.

Two Acts of Parliament are of particular significance:

- The 1944 Education Act, which gave every child an entitlement to free education until the age of 15.
- The 1988 Education Reform Act (ERA), which established a National Curriculum.

There is a requirement to teach RE in community schools

The 1988 ERA (Chapter One section 8) makes the provision of religious education mandatory in all maintained schools (now known as community schools). This was a continuation of the 1944 Act. Children have an entitlement to RE unless the parents exercise their right to withdraw them (see below). Children should thus not be taken from RE for extra lessons in reading or any other activity, however worthwhile.

The curriculum is set at a local rather than a national level

Although RE is part of the basic curriculum, if you look in your National Curriculum you will NOT find a section on RE there. Instead your statutory curriculum document is a **Local Agreed Syllabus**. This syllabus is determined at a local authority level at a Local Syllabus Conference convened by a committee set up by the **Standing Advisory Council for Religious Education (SACRE)**. SACREs meet regularly to oversee and support RE in the local authority and must, by law, review the syllabus every five years. A SACRE is comprised of four groups representing the Church of England, other religions and other Christian denominations, the council and teachers.

The RE curriculum is determined at a local level because this practice was already in place at the time of the 1988 ERA. Before 1988 all schools determined their own curriculum; what they taught in English, maths and science was completely up to the individual school or even teacher. The one exception was Religious Instruction; maintained schools had to follow a Local Agreed Syllabus. This was an indication of the sensitivity at the time surrounding what should be taught to children about faith and religion. The content had to be agreed by the community and not just left to the individual teacher.

At the time of the 1988 Act and the birth of a curriculum set at national level Parliament decided to maintain the status quo rather than set a National Curriculum for RE, a decision which some have since regretted. It means that there are as many syllabuses for RE as there are local authorities. An unfortunate consequence of this local location of the syllabus is that

RE is often side-lined in school because it isn't in the National Curriculum. Nevertheless, it is just as much a legal requirement as any other area of the curriculum.

There are, however, three significant differences between the 1944 Act and the 1988 Act. Under the 1944 Act religion in school was referred to as RI: Religious Instruction. The 1988 act changed the word 'instruction' to 'education'. Government circular 1/94 further reinforced the idea that RE was education, with the decree that Agreed Syllabuses *must not be designed to convert pupils or to urge a particular religion or religious belief on pupils*. (DfE, 1994, p15).

REFLECTIVE TASK

Analyse the difference between instruction and education. What are the implications for the way you teach RE?

Secondly, an Agreed Syllabus shall *reflect the fact that the religious traditions in Great Britain are in the main Christian while taking account of the teaching and practices of the other principal religions represented in Great Britain*. (DfE, 1994, p45)

The explicit reference to Christianity has been perhaps the most controversial aspect of the law. Christianity was not mentioned in the 1944 Act because there was an assumption that Religious Instruction would be Christian. However, significant studies by Loukes (1961) and Goldman (1964) suggested that children were not understanding the subject matter and were finding it irrelevant. As a consequence, from the early 1970s onwards there was a move away from the Bible-based syllabuses of earlier years to syllabuses that prepared children for the understanding of religious concepts and then in later years to syllabuses that embraced the increasingly multicultural society. Rather than being a sharing of one faith, some syllabuses became the examination of world-views. These shifts brought about a backlash among those who were concerned that children were failing to understand the Christian cultural and religious heritage and who feared that a national identity would be lost. Their lobbying ensured that an explicit reference was made to Christianity in the new act. The justification for the predominance of Christianity was largely a cultural one rather than to do with the RE.

REFLECTIVE TASK

List evidence that Christianity is the religion which has had the most influence on this country. Think of the landscape, history, festivals, rites of passage and the Arts. What do you think children need to know and understand in order to have an understanding of this society?

The third significant change is that the law made explicit for the first time that all children should learn about the other principal religions practised in Great Britain. It thus recognised and valued the increasing presence of people of non-Christian religions in the UK, an indication of a hope that knowledge and understanding would also lead to mutual respect between members of different faiths.

The current guidance to SACREs is that Christianity should be studied at each key stage whereas the other religions must be studied in the course of a school career. The Non-

Statutory National Framework for RE (QCA, 2004) also encourages teachers to draw on the religious backgrounds of children in their classes from smaller religions such as the Bahai faith and from non-faith perspectives.

The other principal religions studied are not prescribed by law but are generally held to be Buddhism, Hinduism, Islam, Judaism and Sikhism. There is an introduction to each of these religions at the back of this book.

The changes outlined above were specific to RE. The 1988 Act also introduced a requirement for the whole curriculum that it should: *promote the spiritual, moral, cultural, mental and physical [SMCMP] development of pupils at the school and of society* (Ch. 1, ERA, 1988). SMCMP is a duty of the whole curriculum but has special resonance for RE. Chapter 5 of this book pays particular attention to it.

The right of withdrawal from RE

Parents have the right to withdraw their children from RE. If a parent asks for a child to be withdrawn from RE try to have an open discussion with him or her about the nature of their objections or if you don't feel confident enough to do this, refer the parent to the head teacher.

Many teachers are understandably concerned when parents ask for a child to be withdrawn from RE, especially since it suggests that the parents are not willing for their child to learn and respect viewpoints other than their own. The most common group requesting withdrawal is the Jehovah's Witnesses, who do not permit the observation of festivals, including birthdays. There is also a concern that children will feel excluded if asked to leave the classroom. This is ultimately the parents' choice and there are no neat answers to the problem. However, you can give the child something to do which is related to the subject under discussion. Example: ask the child to write a story on the theme of good overcoming evil when doing Diwali. Or try to think of an unobtrusive positive way of enabling them to be absent from the class.

CASE STUDY

A Year 2 teacher was concerned about the fact that a shy Jehovah's Witness child would feel further excluded during her RE lessons so she arranged that the child should be made a special helper in the Nursery; her time in the Nursery just happened to coincide with RE lessons. She also held non-religious celebrations of the seasons so the child could join in.

You also have the right to be excused from teaching RE on the grounds of conscience. We hope that after reading this book you will see that you can teach RE without being unfaithful to your own beliefs and values. However, if you really feel that you must exercise your right to decline it is your professional duty to inform the head teacher. The children have an entitlement, whatever your views are.

RE in voluntary aided schools (faith schools)

There is one more area regarding the law which you need to understand before you can be fully aware of your professional responsibilities. In order to understand the legal status of RE it is necessary to be fully aware of the distinction between maintained state (community) schools and voluntary aided (faith) schools in the UK. State schools are fully maintained by the state and hence are also known as maintained schools or, since 1998, community schools. Community schools are operated and established by local authorities (county councils). There are also various types of voluntary schools – voluntary aided and voluntary controlled. It is voluntary aided schools which are our concern here. These schools are jointly funded by the state and a religious body.

Most of these voluntary aided (faith) schools are Christian church schools, mainly Church of England (CofE) or Roman Catholic (RC), though there are some long-established Jewish schools. The Labour government in the 1990s extended voluntary status to what were previously private schools rooted in traditions other than Christian and Jewish, most notably Muslim communities. Since 1997 Muslim, Sikh and Hindu schools have also joined the voluntary aided sector. Many religious schools do admit children from other religions and indeed some parents prefer their children to go to a school where there is a high respect for the life of faith and belief in God, even if it is not their own religion. A number of CofE schools in the inner cities have a very high percentage of Muslim children. Clergy are usually very respectful of the religious integrity of the children and seek to build bridges between faiths rather than impose their own religion on the children.

If you teach in a voluntary aided school you will NOT follow the Local Agreed Syllabus. Instead you will follow the religious syllabus set by the school or the funding body. The Roman Catholic Church and Church of England have diocesan syllabuses. Although these syllabuses are usually premised on the truth of the claims made by the faith, some do have some teaching about other religions in order to encourage respect and harmony.

Not all schools with a religious title are voluntary aided. Some are fully in the maintained sector and are voluntary controlled. These schools follow the Local Agreed Syllabus.

REFLECTIVE TASK

Think about why parents or guardians would choose to send their child to a 'faith school'. What are the arguments for and against faith schools?

The aims of RE

It is very important that you understand the educational aims of all the subjects that you teach, so that you teach them in a manner that addresses these aims. Strictly speaking, each local SACRE is able to determine its own aims and objectives for RE so long as they are within the 1988 Act. These are set out in the front of your Local Agreed Syllabus. However, the Qualifications and Curriculum Authority (QCA) and central government have issued a number of documents to guide local SACREs when they review their Agreed Syllabuses. Among these documents were the Model Syllabuses (SCAA, 1994), which were two models for SACREs to follow if they wished to do so when writing their local syllabus. These model syllabuses were drawn up in wide consultation with members of different religions. They offered the following aims for RE which were reiterated in the QCA's 2004 Non-Statutory Framework for RE.

RE aims to help children to:

- acquire and develop knowledge and understanding of Christianity and other principal religions represented in the United Kingdom;
- develop an understanding of the influence of beliefs, values and traditions on individuals, communities, society and cultures;
- develop the ability to make reasoned judgements about religious and moral issues with reference to principal religions represented in the United Kingdom;
- enhance their spiritual, moral, social and cultural development;
- develop positive attitudes towards other people, respecting their right to hold different beliefs from one's own, and towards living in a society of diverse religions.

These aims acknowledge the importance religion has in the lives of many individuals throughout the world and also the impact of those beliefs on the whole of culture and society. This assumes that a general aim for education is that children understand the world in which they live, including religion.

Finally, RE has an explicit objective of helping to maintain a harmonious society. This last point has been reconfirmed in a recent report from OFSTED entitled *Making sense of Religion* (2007), which stated clearly that RE in schools has new responsibilities to promote social cohesion:

> *Those with responsibility for RE therefore have the task of ensuring that children and young people are able to make sense of religion in the modern world and issues of identity and diversity.*

Attainment Targets in RE

The aims of the subjects of the Basic Curriculum are developed into Attainment Targets to help shape the curriculum, but once again in RE these are determined at a local rather than a national level. However, Model Syllabuses advised that a Local Agreed Syllabus should have two Attainment Targets for RE:

- AT1 Learning about Religion;
- AT2 Learning from Religion.

In this book we make reference to these two Attainment Targets as they are widely used in Agreed Syllabuses. However, as they are not statutory, syllabuses may express and interpret them in slightly different ways. Hampshire, unusually, has only one Attainment Target: *interpreting religion in relation to human experience*.

Attainment Target 1: Learning about Religion

This is concerned with:

- enquiry into, and investigation of, the nature of religion, its beliefs, teachings and ways of life, sources, practices and forms of expression;
- the skills of interpretation, analysis and explanation. Children learn to communicate their knowledge and understanding using specialist vocabulary;
- identifying and developing an understanding of ultimate questions and ethical issues;
- values and commitment.

Attainment Target 2: Learning from Religion

This is concerned with:

- developing children's reflection on and response to their own and others' perceptions and experiences in the light of their learning about religion;
- developing children's skills of application, interpretation and evaluation of what they will learn about religion.

Children learn to develop and communicate their own ideas particularly in relation to questions of identity and belonging, meaning, purpose and truth.

Underpinning the idea of learning from religion is the fundamental idea that religions are an expression of a desire for meaning and purpose in life. People seek answers to questions such as *Why do good people suffer?* or *Is there a God?* and *What's the point of living?* For many religious people that meaning and purpose has been revealed by God in a holy book or person. For others the quest for meaning and purpose is part of life's journey – there are no complete answers, though some answers may be better than others. That meaning and purpose is as likely to be found in engagement with ritual, or being part of a community, as in assent to a set of teachings.

Of course, there are many millions of people who find meaning and purpose outside the world of religion, in the communities they belong to, and in the values they hold. Community schools as well as faith schools often give children a strong sense of belonging and identity, valuing them as individuals. Teachers can convey to children a huge sense that life is worth living. Moreover, religions don't have all the answers, which is perhaps why the Birmingham Agreed Syllabus of 1975 included Marxism as a world-view and the Humanist Society is pressing for Humanism to be included in RE. Moreover, some traditional teachings and practice may be challenged by a changing morality. There is a clash, for example, between attitudes to women and to homosexuality, as found in some religious teachings, and a growth towards equality, inclusion and respect for individual choice, as found in the law.

A lot of spontaneous discussion in the classroom perhaps in response to a book, or something seen on television, is about such questions. However, RE is the place where you should plan to ensure that such discussions happen because the religions deal with these questions of meaning. In RE we encourage children to think about themselves and the implications of what they are studying for their lives.

The **learning from** aspect of RE has been welcomed by some teachers but perceived by others as difficult. Whereas learning about the facts and ways of life of various religious cultures is relatively easy to plan and deliver, enabling children to understand their own beliefs and values more deeply and also reflect upon them, is a real challenge. Yet it is here that RE can most contribute to children's development as whole people who make active, thoughtful contributions to society.

RE teachers face this challenge constantly. It is often simpler for them to fall back on the mechanics of religion instead of tackling the reality of being religious. Textbooks tend to concentrate on ceremonies rather than what it is like to live as a Catholic, a Muslim or a Hindu in the community; and to discuss where values and codes for living come from for children who do not have religious belief. It is an area which needs considerable work if we are to meet our objectives of developing active, articulate, critical learners who understand the value of difference and unity and have the ability to participate and engage in current debates.

(DfES, 2007)

However learning from religion can provide opportunities for holistic approaches to learning, which included emotional and moral dimensions and can contribute to the personal, moral and spiritual development of the child. This is particularly apparent in the attitudes developed through RE which are defined in the National Framework as self awareness, respect for all, open-mindedness, appreciation and wonder. (DfES, 2007).

Suggestions on how to integrate Learning about Religion with Learning from Religion are made throughout this book.

The structure of Local Agreed Syllabuses

The fact that the syllabus is designed locally gives variety and flexibility to the content and structure of RE. Some SACREs appoint a working group of teachers who develop this local syllabus. Some have extensive consultations with members of the local communities, including religious leaders. One of the consequences of the local nature of the RE syllabuses is that there can be huge differences between them. These differences lie not only in which religions are covered at each stage but in the manner of organisation.

For example, the Hampshire Agreed Syllabus is built around key concepts whereas the Manchester Agreed Syllabus, uses such themes as Growing Up in a Christian family in Key Stage 1, Special People in Years 3 and 4, and Special Books, and The Journey of Life in Years 5 and 6. The content which supports and exemplifies each of these themes reflects the multicultural nature of the communities in Manchester.

The organisation of Agreed Syllabuses tends to fall into two main types.

- **Systematic approaches** consider each world religion separately as a discrete unit with distinctive features. The strength of this approach is that it means children are more likely to have a sound basis of knowledge in each religion. The drawback is that they learn to see religions in little boxes and may fail to make connections between them.
- **Thematic approaches** take a key feature of religion such as worship, rites of passage, special books or sacred places, and seek to explore the nature and purpose of this feature across various religions. This has the advantage of helping children see connections but the disadvantage that each religion may not be understood in its own right. Themes such as environmental awareness and citizenship may be drawn from the cross-curricular themes (see Chapter 5).

Remember that it is the Local Agreed Syllabus which is the statutory document NOT the units of study for RE on the QCA Website. These units are a helpful resource as you plan RE but should not be followed slavishly; the variance between Agreed Syllabuses means that it is impossible to create a sequence of units that matches all Agreed Syllabuses.

PRACTICAL TASK PRACTICAL TASK PRACTICAL TASK PRACTICAL TASK PRACTICAL TASK

Look at the Local Agreed Syllabus for your area or for a school in which you are teaching. Compare its Aims and Attainment Targets with those found in the Model Syllabuses. Look at how the curriculum is organised. Compare the programme of study with the units of study found on the QCA Website.

From syllabus to school

Community schools are at liberty to plan their RE themselves so long as they cover the content of the Local Agreed Syllabus, including its skills. Thus the material in the syllabus may be organised around discrete religions, but the school may decide to deliver it in a cross-curricular way integrating it with other curriculum areas and other cross-curricular themes such as citizenship. Some local authorities provide more detailed programmes of study than others.

CASE STUDY

The RE co-ordinator was discussing the programme of study in the Agreed Syllabus with a Year 1 teacher. The study of Islam was one unit in the Local Agreed Syllabus. Most of the children were Muslim. They decided that instead of studying Islam as a separate subject they would integrate it with curriculum areas in recognition of how important it was in children's lives. Thus in a topic on water and its uses they decided to look at washing hands before prayer. In a unit on time they would look at prayer times for the day and when the special Friday prayers were. They were covering the content required but in a way that was relevant to the children in the class.

For more on cross-curricular planning see Chapter 2.

RE and collective worship

RE should not be confused with school collective worship. They are two separate entities. You are responsible for RE in your class unless other arrangements are made. It is the head teacher's or in the case of voluntary aided schools the chair of governors' responsibility to see that a daily act of worship takes place in the school. This worship should be *wholly or mainly of a broadly Christian character* unless the school has applied for exemption because it has a large number of children from another religion. This is a controversial law open to wide interpretation but legally school collective worship does not have any more link with RE than with any other subject area. A Muslim festival of Eid can be marked in an act of worship in a joyful way and on the occasion be reinforcing RE, but then a favourite author's birthday can also be celebrated. Poetry and music can be brought together for a theme on the weather, thus making a link with geography; children can share their excitement and knowledge about a history topic.

However, good school collective worship can supplement RE in that it can give children experiences of community, shared joys and times of sorrow, awe and wonder which can be drawn on later in an RE lesson. An act of worship based on the life of a hero-figure such as Mary Seacole could be followed up with an RE lesson on different types of bravery.

Also, you can use short times at the end of the day to give children a sense of the sacred and ensure the day ends on a positive note in a time akin to collective worship. As well as the pleasure of sharing a book together, or communal singing (not necessarily religious stories or songs), you might celebrate some of the good things of the day with a cheer and a clap and you might remember by lighting a candle those children who are absent.

REFLECTIVE TASK

To check your understanding of your professional responsibilities decide why these community schools are NOT observing the law.

- School A only teaches about Christianity because all the children in the school come from a culturally Christian background.
- School B doesn't teach Christianity at all because all the children are from a Muslim background.
- School C follows the QCA units of work for RE; no-one has looked at the Local Agreed Syllabus in years.
- School D doesn't have separate RE lessons, the children just have moral stories in assembly.

RE, creativity and this book

Two major government reports in the last decade have promoted creativity in schools: *All Our Futures* (DfES, 1999) and *Excellence and Enjoyment* (DfES, 2003). This book attempts to reflect those reports in the approach we have taken to RE. We would encourage you to be a creative teacher – a teacher who is prepared to think imaginatively and employs drama, art and music and makes links with other subjects to make learning interesting and engaging for the children. However, whereas creativity is usually associated with originality, you do not need to be original except in the sense of being prepared to move outside your comfort zone, and take risks and try out new ideas wherever you have gathered them from; that way you will keep your teaching of RE alive and invigorating. Creativity also involves fit for purpose – your creative activities should further the aims of RE not detract from them.

We would also encourage you to teach for creativity. Good RE gives children the space to put something of themselves in it and use their imagination whether in reflection, analysis or a practical activity. We would discourage your use of worksheets, cloze procedure and word searches and instead exhort you to use open-ended activities that encourage personal response. There are lots of suggestions in the book to help you do that.

REFLECTIVE TASK

Look back to your notes about the RE you had at school. What approach was taken? What was emphasised? Did you learn about different religions? Were you given the opportunity to explore religious ideas? Do you think your school obeyed the law? Was RE taught as a creative subject?

Conclusion

This chapter has introduced you to the unique position of RE in British education law. Do remember to use your Local Agreed Syllabus or in a faith school the one provided by the relevant religion as your curriculum guidance. You should make reference to this in your teaching plans. The rest of the book is guidance on how to implement that law in a creative way that promotes children's thinking and learning.

A SUMMARY OF **KEY POINTS**

> The 1988 Education Act gives every child an entitlement to RE.

> The RE syllabus is determined at a local authority level by an SACRE.

> A study of Christianity and the practices of the other principal religions in the UK must be included in the Syllabus.

> There is a conscience clause for children and teachers giving a right of withdrawal from RE.

> Faith schools have a syllabus for RE set by the relevant religious authority.

> The aims of RE make it more than the study of religion.

> There are usually two Attainment Targets for RE: Learning about Religion and Learning from Religion.

> Schools can deliver the content of a Local Agreed Syllabus in their own way.

> School collective worship and RE are not the same thing.

> Let's be creative about RE.

MOVING *ON* > > > > > > MOVING *ON* > > > > > > MOVING *ON*

Find out the following things about the school you are working in or in which you are doing your placement.

● Is it a community (maintained) school with a Local Agreed Syllabus or is it a 'faith' school with a syllabus determined by the relevant religion?

● Does the school's programme of study for RE follow the organisation of the Local Agreed Syllabus or has it been reorganised?

● What sort of status does RE have in the school? Is the importance of learning from religion recognised?

2
Encountering religion: issues and principles

Chapter objectives

By the end of this chapter you will have developed knowledge and understanding of:

- **the breadth of religion;**
- **issues in the study of religion with children;**
- **key pedagogical principles in studying religion with children.**

This chapter addresses the following Standards for QTS: **Q14, Q18, Q19**

Introduction

As we saw in Chapter 1, the 1988 Education Reform Act made explicit that Christianity and the other principal religions of the United Kingdom must be taught in all local authority schools. It is the responsibility of each local authority to determine which religion(s) should be taught at which key stage according to local conditions (see Chapter 1). Whether or not other religions are taught in a faith school will depend on the relevant religious body.

You will no doubt be feeling a little anxious about your own subject knowledge regarding the teaching of religion, fearing that you could be walking through mine fields and being concerned that you won't offend. This chapter is essentially about helping you find an appropriate route to help children meet and engage with religious life and practice. The chapter is divided into three sections:

- What is religion?
- Issues in teaching about religions;
- Basic pedagogical principles.

What is religion?

In the 1960s Professor Ninian Smart pioneered an approach to answering this question which has remained a major influence on the writing of Agreed Syllabuses, although thinking in RE has moved on from the pedagogy of RE that Smart created. It is also a very useful framework for considering what RE encompasses. Rather than looking to the etymology of the word religion or debating philosophical definitions of it, Smart sought to describe the phenomenon that is religion by considering its dimensions, developing and modifying them over the years.

Ninian Smart's seven dimensions of religion

Smart's dimensions are presented here as cited in Bastide (1992, p191), with our commentary.

1 The practical and ritual dimension
Those aspects of religious life which are visible and often involve order and symbolic action. This dimension includes daily rituals in the home such as the saying of a blessing before a meal, communal rituals such as sharing the bread and wine at communion in Christian church, yearly rituals associated with festivals, and rites of passage from birth to death.

2 The experiential and emotional dimension
Many people have a powerful sense of the presence of God. For some this is an intimate sense of the presence of God in everyday lives; for others the experience of God may be something suddenly extraordinary in a vision or in a revelation. Some find God in solitude, others in a community of believers, some in prayer. But we cannot tie the experiential aspect of religion down to those with this powerful sense. For many the sense of God may be felt as an absence, or they may even feel agnostic about God but find meaning and worth in involvement in a local religious community. Some deeply religious people may even feel uncomfortable with the word God, and prefer to speak of a sense of the transcendence or 'otherness'. Buddhism does not speak of an almighty God at all, though some forms of Buddhism have deities.

William James in his 1902 Gifford Lectures noted the variety of religious experiences which can include people who have the 'religion of healthy mindedness' (Chs 4 and 5), 'those with a sick soul' (Chs 6 and 7), and 'mystics' (Chs 16, 17). Across religions we may find differences in teachings and rituals but people who have much in common in the way they believe. There are those who have very fixed fundamentalist views in most religions, those who are liberal in their outlook, and those who emphasise the spiritual and mystical dimensions of the religion.

3 The narrative and the mythic dimension
All religions have stories, which may range from grand myths about the beginning of time, stories about the founders and heroes of the religion, to teaching parables. Some of these narratives may have taken place in real time, others definitely are mythic in character. For a closer discussion on the range of religious literature see Chapter 4.

4 The doctrinal and the philosophical dimension
All religions have some basic teachings, often called doctrine. For example: Islam has a strict belief in the oneness and unity of God, the concept of non-attachment is a key teaching in Buddhism, and the presence of God in Jesus is a central belief in Christianity.

The philosophical dimension embraces the questions of meaning which are explored in AT2 Learning about Religion and seem to rise out of the nature of being human – questions such as *Who am I? What happens after death? Why do the good suffer?*

5 The ethical and the legal dimension
All religions have an ethical dimension usually, but not necessarily, encoded in religious law. Sometimes this law stretches beyond the moral law to include ritual law. For example Orthodox Judaism adheres to the Ten Commandments and also has strict rules about the preparation of food. Within the one religion you will find those who have a strict rigid adherence to laws, while others may give primacy to compassion and love over particular laws.

6 The social and institutional dimensions

While for some people religion is a strictly private matter and a question of personal belief, worship and prayer with others, discussion about the meaning of text and the celebration of festivals are essential to the religious life. The social part often extends beyond the explicitly religious rituals into charity work and social gathering. For example: the langar – the Sikh free kitchen where everyone comes to eat after the services; some Christians meet together for regular Bible study.

All religious movements eventually become institutionalised or they wither and die. They have leaders who may also have priestly and/or pastoral responsibilities. They may have bodies who are responsible for determining which teachings correctly interpret the religion. Some religious groups such as the Christian house church movement are very independent, with loose associations with other like-minded people. Others are part of a much bigger organisation which emphasises the historical chain taking them back to the origins of the religion. For example: the Roman Catholic Church has one major world leader, the Pope, and claims a history of succession back to the first apostles in the early Christian church.

7 The material dimension

Religions abound with objects from prayer beads carried in the pocket, to the way people dress, to mighty buildings. Judaism and Islam forbid the use of images of living people in prayer and worship but nevertheless have a strong tradition of abstract art. (Many Protestant Christians also eschew images in places of worship.) On the other hand, the use of imagery in worship is very important to Roman Catholic Christians, Orthodox Christians and Hindus.

These seven dimensions inter-relate. A cathedral is a religious object but it is also a place of social and ritual events. The stained glass windows in cathedrals often tell the story of Jesus and holy people in Christianity. It may have a room for putting into practice the Christian ethic of charity by serving the poor. The main doctrines (teachings) of Christianity will be expressed in the saying of the creed (a statement of belief) during the services.

Or to take another example: the belief held by Muslims that the Qur'an is God's final revelation to humanity is expressed in rituals about care of the Holy Book (Dimensions 1 and 7); the story of that revelation and narratives within the Qur'an (Dimension 3); the principles of Islamic ethics (Dimension 6) are found in the Qur'an.

Study of religions involves studying all these dimensions; RE is not confined to any single dimension but covers them all. A religious education that only concentrated on the moral dimension would be too narrow as would one that only looked at stories. However, at Key Stage 1 explicit study of religion tends to concentrate on those aspects that are visible and concrete.

PRACTICAL TASK PRACTICAL TASK PRACTICAL TASK PRACTICAL TASK PRACTICAL TASK

To develop your subject knowledge start either a paper or electronic folder in which you gather information about each world religion using the seven dimensions as sub-headings. Use the Appendix at the back of this book as a starting point.

Issues in teaching about religions

One of your roles as a teacher is help children develop the skills to make sense of their world and the world introduced to them by you. In order to do that in the world of religion in all its breadth you need to be aware of some basic issues for yourself and in the discussion about teaching it.

Issue1: knowing where you are starting from

Anthropologists and other students of religions have increasingly recognised the importance of knowing ourselves when we study religion and when we teach others to study religion. Each one of us will have experiences of religion, positive or negative, whether or not we belong to a faith community. Each one of us has beliefs, fears and hopes, even if very vague, whether or not these include belief in God. Those experiences and beliefs will inevitably shape the way we approach the teaching of the explicitly religious content of RE. Strong convictions, or even unquestioned assumptions in the truth of our own faith position, may lead us to unintentionally promote our own faith position and/or be subtly dismissive or disparaging about the beliefs and practices of others; 'I have true beliefs – others have superstitions.'

REFLECTIVE TASK

Be honest with yourself about your beliefs and attitudes to religion. How might these affect your approach to the teaching of the subject?

Issue 2: but I don't believe that!

Hannah declared loudly in the staffroom that she didn't believe in God so she wasn't going to teach about God. Hannah thinks that RE teaches children about God. It does not. RE is the place where children learn what different people believe about God and explore their own beliefs. It does not assume the existence of God.

You need to find a way of teaching about religion that is honest to your own beliefs. An atheist can teach that Islam teaches that there is one God, without believing herself that God exists. A Muslim can teach that the Bible calls Jesus the son of God even though he believes that God has no sons and Jesus is a prophet.

Teachers often worry about children asking them about their beliefs: 'What do you think happens after death, Miss?' There is a right concern about unwittingly imposing a view on the child because children often look to the teacher as a figure of authority. The best way of answering is to be honest and if possible to return the question to the child. Acknowledge your own belief but also acknowledge other viewpoints and ask the children for their ideas.

However, not every religious item is a matter of personal faith and conviction. Taking an honest approach will also mean that you need to learn to differentiate between items that are factual, in that they are uncontested by the majority of people and are open to historical enquiry, and items that are matters of faith and belief.

Look at the following list and put Fact or Faith next to each one. What are your reasons? Have a discussion with someone from a different faith background about them.

- Jesus had his ministry approximately 2000 years ago in the region now known as Israel.
- Jesus rose again from the dead.
- Muhammad was born in Makkah (Mecca) in Saudi Arabia.
- The angel Jibra'eel (Gabriel) revealed the Qur'an to Muhammad.
- The Torah is central to Jewish belief and practice.
- Hinduism is widely practised in India.
- After death we will be reincarnated.

Issue 3: The religious backgrounds of children in your class

Children of the faith under study are a rich resource. RE may be a time when they have all the thrill of being the authority, of even perhaps knowing more than the teacher. But you will need to be tactful and sensitive in your approach. Be careful about asking a child directly about their faith unless you have strong evidence to indicate they are happy with this. The child may not know THE answer and then may feel embarrassed or he may not want to share his experiences. Instead leave the space open for children to come forward to share their experiences and beliefs, and they usually do. Remember too that the child will be bringing his particular experience of his religion, which may differ from the mainstream or even from another child in the class (see p19, Start with the particular).

Be prepared for the convictions of the children in your class having an impact on discussions. You may, for example, find children from particular faith backgrounds coming to school with a strong, and maybe to you, shocking antipathy to the study of religions or convictions about their own.

CASE STUDY

Mrs Johnson was quite shocked when one of her Muslim children declared his millennium wish to be that he wanted the world to convert to Islam. She took it as a form of racism and intolerance. She had not understood that the prayers for conversion would have been a daily part of the prayers in the child's home, just as this is a regular practice among many Christians. Many a kindly Christian and Muslim will pray for conversions because they want to share what they believe to be the truth and what has brought meaning into their lives, although their day-to-day practice is one of tolerance and an acceptance that individuals should come to these conclusions themselves.

Do some background reading on the religions of children in your class. How may this background affect your teaching? Follow it up with an activity in which children draw or write about things that are important to their family. This may help you gain insight into their family backgrounds and whether or not religious observance is important to the child. It will help you achieve Standard Q18: *Understand how children and young people develop and that the progress and well-being of learners are affected by a range of developmental, social, religious, ethnic, cultural and linguistic influences*.

Issue 4: the fear of mishmash – an issue for long-term planning

There has been a long debate in RE as to whether religions should be introduced to children as discrete units, or whether the study of religion should be part of a cross-curricular programme linked with subjects such as history, geography or art. The arguments for a cross-curricular approach to RE are those that are counter to the approach which takes discrete units. We will look at the arguments from the cross-curricular perspective.

There are four main reasons for taking a cross-curricular approach in introducing children to religions.

- They will understand that religion is an integral part of life not something distinct from the rest of you. *Example:* In thinking about what goes on in a home children can learn that prayer and worship is one activity.
- They will see the connections between different subject areas. *Example:* To study India in geography without studying Hinduism is to miss a major aspect of Indian life. Identity is a subject explored in both RE and Art.
- They will learn to see that different subject areas bring different sets of questions, and different responses to the same topic. *Example:* A topic on my home with Key Stage 1 could include:
  - historical questions: How long have I lived here? How old is my house? What changes have been made to it?
  - geographical questions: Where is my home? How do I get from my house to school? What is the ground plan of my house?
  - scientific questions: What is electricity used for in my house?
  - religious questions: What is special about my home? How do I celebrate in my home?
  Some questions of course have answers that cross the boundaries. For example, What do I do in my home? includes health (sleep, eat) but may also include value (spend time with my family) and explicitly religious activities (praying, making offerings to a shrine, reading the sacred text).
- It is economic use of curriculum time when time is short. *Example:* The understanding of the symbolism of light is important to understanding festivals of light and the metaphor of light. The study of light is obviously also an important part of science. It makes sense to do the study together.

There are, however, disadvantages in taking a cross-curricular approach.

- Children end up with a mishmash of information from various religions and become very confused.
- Key aspects of a religion and key skills in studying religion are overlooked because they don't fit in with the topic covered.
- The same content is returned to repeatedly. This used to happen particularly with the story of Noah which was used in topics on home, colour, transport, weather, wood and many more.
- Sudden reference to an aspect of religion does not make sense to children because they have no context for it. For example, suddenly saying to children that many Sikhs wear turbans in a topic on hats can be meaningless if the children have not come across the word Sikh before.

Good planning does, however, make it possible to have the best of both worlds. Plan discrete units of work to introduce children to a religion but draw on examples from religions the children have studied before in cross-curricular topics.

CASE STUDY

Michelle Edwards knew that the children in her Year 3 class had learnt about Christianity, Hinduism and Islam during Key Stage 1. She therefore planned a unit of work around the theme of the Torah in the first term as a means of introducing her children to Judaism. She made the following links with other topics throughout the year.

- A science-led topic on light and shadows in November: festivals of light in Hinduism, Judaism and Christianity.
- A geography-led topic on investigating our local area. The children mapped the buildings used for worship in the area around the school and visited the synagogue where they looked at how the Torah was treasured.
- A geography-led topic on weather around the world. The children looked at pilgrimage being a reason for travel and researched the weather in the places of pilgrimage for the religions they had studied.
- A maths-led topic on time: in one lesson the children read the Muslim prayer times for the day.
- A history-led topic on the Roman Invasion: an examination of Roman ideas about God. How do they compare with ideas about God held in Hinduism and Islam?

In taking this approach this teacher has helped the children make connections with prior learning and between their learning in different subject areas.

Some basic pedagogical principles

Have a secure knowledge and understanding of their subjects/curriculum areas and related pedagogy to enable them to teach effectively across the age and ability range for which they are trained.

(Q14)

There is a constant debate in all subjects about what constitutes appropriate pedagogy and RE is no exception. Discussions about the best way to teach RE draw on research in the area of religious studies as well as research in the classroom but the resultant pedagogies often reflect the particular understanding of faith and interests of the proponent. Thus Robert Jackson's work reflects his interests in ethnography, David Hay's his interest in the experiential aspects of religion, and Trevor Cooling's work reflects his commitment to theology as a discipline. (See Michael Grimmitt's book *Pedagogies of RE* (2000) for introductions to these and other approaches.) The following principles draw on these debates and their pedagogies, in particular the pedagogy of Jackson and the pedagogy of the 'Gift to the Child' religion in the service of the child project (Grimmitt et al., 1999).

Pedagogical principle 1: remember the child

In all the discussion about RE and concerns about ways of approaching the subject it is important to remember that at the heart of education lies the child. RE extends the children's experience and enlarges their understanding of the world but unless you are responding to children's needs, questions and comments, recognising them as learners finding meaning, you will miss the point. All your objectives are secondary to responding to children.

Pedagogical principle 2: start with the particular and help children see connections

There are two important reasons why the study of a religion with children needs to begin with particular instances of the religion rather than sweeping general statements.

First, all religions are diverse in their belief and practice. While there may be some central beliefs and practices held in common, there are still differences in interpretation. So, for example, baptism is a core ritual in Christianity, but not only is there the division between those churches who baptise children as infants and those who only baptise as adults, but the beliefs and details of the baptism will vary. The one thing in common is the use of water as a central part of the ritual. Or, to take another example, while many Sikhs do not cut their hair, and place a very big emphasis on the Khalsa, some Sikhs do not and prioritise the teaching and life of the first Guru. It is not just a matter of trying not to misrepresent the faith but is important in avoiding disturbing children of the faith in the class. Muslim children have been known to be upset at being told that Muslims pray five times a day when they know that in their family people only pray three times. One child wrote that she didn't like RE because it made her feel like a bad Muslim.

Secondly children learn best with the concrete and the particular. Judaism is an abstract concept, talking about Jews observing Passover is too distant and cold, but describing young Sam excitedly getting ready for the Passover, now that is another matter.

The implication for your planning is that you build your RE units around a particular child or family, especially at Key Stage 1. Rather than learning about Judaism children can learn about a child growing up in a Jewish family. Then any Jewish children in the class can claim the amount of similarity and difference that is appropriate to their own experience. In order to do this successfully, you may need to build a narrative from lesson to lesson around a Jewish (Hindu, Muslim, etc) child in a photograph or you can use a doll giving it an appropriate name. Thus you can think about what Sam is allowed to eat when visiting a restaurant, and what he does on a Friday evening, etc. You can create awareness of diversity by giving Sam a cousin who comes from a stricter family and doesn't visit restaurants at all. A word of warning: do not give a puppet or doll the name Muhammad as this might be regarded as disrespectful to the prophet, even though Muslim boys are often called Muhammad.

While creating a family for older Key Stage 2 children may be excessively artificial it is still better to think about the particular, for example How are the Torah scrolls looked after in this particular synagogue? What do these blessings say about an attitude to the environment? Then explore with children how these encounters with the particulars of a religion fit together with other knowledge gained.

If you find yourself talking about Christians, Jews, etc. do talk about 'most' Christians or 'some' Jews so as to avoid the impression that everyone belonging to the faith does what you are describing exactly as you describe it.

> **PRACTICAL TASK** PRACTICAL TASK PRACTICAL TASK PRACTICAL TASK PRACTICAL TASK
>
> Find an image of a child from a religion you know little about. Write a story about the daily life of that child including what she/he enjoys at school, who she/he plays with. Weave into the story a description of the child's home with its rituals and celebrations. You will of course need to do some background reading to fulfil the task.

Pedagogical principle 3: look for similarities between the children's experience and the specific religious experience

In all teaching it is generally good teaching practice to make links with what the children already know when introducing them to something or someone new. This makes the new information more accessible and more meaningful. Drawing out the similarity in a religious practice to something that the children have experienced can help the children gain some sort of grasp on it.

Moreover it could be argued that a major root of many evil acts is a failure by the perpetrator to recognise and care that the enemy or victim is also a human being, whether the victim is an abused child, a victim of a street attack, of a programme of genocide, or standing in the wake of a bomb. It seems instinctively important that we should emphasise similarities when we are introducing children to something outside their own immediate experience.

Many religious practices are analogous to activities in the secular world, the world outside religion. For example, many of us in getting ready to go to a party will put ourselves in the mood for it by washing and dressing up. The process can transform us from feeling tired and out of sorts to being ready to be sociable. The Muslim ritual of washing to be ready for prayer is analogous to this in that it is a transition time, a time of preparation.

The recognition that there are similarities between specific religious practices and practices in secular life will help you find either an entrance point to a religious practice, and or a follow-up activity which makes connections with children's everyday lives. For example, a lesson on a Muslim child doing Wudu washing for prayer might be preceded by concept mapping with the children when they wash and why. Does having a bath or dressing up to go somewhere special make them feel different? Or when introducing the mezuzah, the small box many Jews fix to the side of their doorways (see Judaism in the Appendix), you might begin by looking at different things the children do when they want to remember to do something or take something somewhere.

This process creates opportunities for children to think about and reflect on their own lives and can also give space for children to value their own home lives and background.

> **PRACTICAL TASK** PRACTICAL TASK PRACTICAL TASK PRACTICAL TASK PRACTICAL TASK
>
> Read up on the following religious phenomena. What links can you make between them and your own experience.
>
> - The Buddhist ritual of bowing to a stupa (statue of the Buddha) is a sign of deep respect for the teachings of the Buddha. How do you show respect to people and teachings?
> - The wearing of special collars, known as dog collars by Christian ministers and priests identifies them as priests. What other clothing is worn to show identity?

- The Hindu ritual of washing and dressing the statue of the god (murti) in a shrine. What objects do you treasure? How do you show you treasure them?
- The Jewish ritual of wrapping oneself in a prayer shawl (tallit) for prayer. What clothing do you wear for special occasions? Why? (Note some Jews describe the wearing of a prayer shawl as being similar to being wrapped in the love of God.)
- The Muslim pilgrimage to Mecca. What places are important to you?
- The Sikh ritual of sharing a sweet mixture (amrit) at the end of worship. When do you give sweet food to others and why?

CASE STUDY

The Year 3 children had been studying the Jewish ritual of Passover. They had learnt a song and eaten some of the bread sprinkled with salt. They were then asked to write about their own special meals. Most wrote about a time when a favourite relative came, or a birthday meal, but Daljit, a hitherto very quiet Sikh boy, wrote about the free communal meal at the Gurdwara. He was then also able to talk at length about it. The advantage of this approach is that children can respond at their own level whatever their achievements in other areas. The differentiation is built into the activity.

In looking at similarities in this way you will be looking at key religious concepts in a concrete way – respect, identity, ritual, pilgrimage, symbols – or in the language of Trevor Cooling (2000), cracking open the concept.

This can be done through talk but also through giving children what Sue Phillips calls 'religion free' rituals with the imaginative use of guided fantasy and drama (see the next chapter). And you are also helping children learn from religion (see Pedagogical principle 5).

Pedagogical principle 4: Also acknowledge difference

An overemphasis on similarity can be counterproductive since it can leave children learning that difference is problematic. When they then encounter difference they may perceive it as necessarily strange and alienating and to be rejected rather than something which might be at the worst tolerable and at the best something life-enhancing.

In the vast majority of instances difference is not only okay but is something which enriches our experiences, enables growth and, with it, learning. Moreover failure to recognise where there is difference can lead to false assumptions. If we mistakenly assume that someone shares our way of viewing the world we may then act inappropriately.

We are not suggesting out and out relativism here, as though anything goes; that can also create a distance between people. We want children to keep their critical antennae well tuned so that they become discerning people. Children need also to learn to see the difference between things which are matters of preference where a huge variety is welcomed, difference regarding interpretation where one might agree to differ, and difference with respect to morality where a common ground might be sought or a compromise made.

Difference can of course be a problem in certain circumstances particularly when it is used as an excuse to lock people into certain roles in a society, or to abuse another. But difference is not in itself a problem and we need to be careful that we don't inadvertently present it to children as one. Think about the following way of making comparisons adapted from a children's book:

Mary has blue eyes. Melody has brown eyes. But they both have a beautiful smile.

And

Mary has blue eyes. Melody has brown eyes. And they both have a beautiful smile.

The use of BUT as a connective makes their differences a problem resolved by their similarity. We can turn this into a specifically religious example.

George goes to church. Imran goes to the mosque. But they both like going to school.

George goes to church. Imran goes to the mosque. And they both like going to school.

Keeping this twin concept of similarity and difference in mind is a very important principle in approaching the study of a religion. Insight into a phenomenon can be gained when children can link an aspect of it to their own experience and see the common humanity. Acknowledging the differences encourages them to accept difference and learn from it. This is the reason a lot of material based on introducing children to a child from a different religion is often based on bringing together similarity and difference.

CASE STUDY

A Year 2 class are watching the Hindu section 'Moon' from a DVD of *Water, Moon, Candle, Tree and Sword* (Channel 4). Afterwards the student teacher asks, How are you similar to the little girl in the DVD? Tom says that he and the girl are both learning to swim. Tessa says that she also has an older brother. Ella says that she has meals with her family. The student teacher then asks how they are different from the child on the DVD. Tessa immediately says that she doesn't make a bracelet for her brother. Mike says they don't have a shrine in his house. Freya adds that she has a statue of the Virgin Mary in her house, but it isn't Hindu. Hanna says she has a photo of a football hero and that's a bit like it. In both instances the teacher draws out the similarity and difference.

We are not suggesting that these rituals are the same – they are similar and different.

Pedagogical principle 5: draw out themes for AT2 Learning from Religion

Studies of religious life and practice (AT1 Learning about Religion) offer many opportunities for AT2 Learning from Religion) because such studies raise many of those all-important questions of meaning. The very act of learning about a child of another faith can lead a child to ask himself, or his parents 'Where do I belong' 'What do we believe in this family?' (at Key Stage 1 children do tend to start with looking to the family for answers to such questions). Learning about birth rituals can create the opportunity for a reflection of values and how parents share them with children; learning about death and bereavement rituals can help children acknowledge the feelings surrounding death and explore the question of what happens when you die. A study of the teachings of Muhammad can be a splendid opportunity for considering responsibilities to animals and moreover having one's own ideas extended and challenged.

Here we see that the identification of similarity can create the opportunity for exploration of a fundamental theme from a new perspective.

PRACTICAL TASK PRACTICAL TASK PRACTICAL TASK PRACTICAL TASK PRACTICAL TASK

Read about the following examples and suggest a question of meaning and purpose for discussion and investigation.

- The Buddhist Sangha (community).
- The Hindu practice of giving a young baby honey as the first food, to represent all that is sweet in life.
- The practice of 'sharing the peace' in many Christian churches.
- Muslims making a pilgrimage for the Hajj.
- The Ten Commandments.
- The Sikh bangle (kara), which, among other things, represents the nature of truth – it can't be broken.

Case Study

A Year 6 class in a suburban school were studying Sikhism. They had heard the story of the founding of the Khalsa and were then asked to work in groups to discuss who or what needed protecting in modern society. One group decided that old people needed protecting but Richard raised the point that some elderly people get annoyed if they are fussed over. This led to an interesting discussion among the children about ways of treating elderly people. Thus they were thinking about the dignity of persons.

Pedagogical principle 6: seek to engage head, heart and hand

RE cannot always be fun – indeed there are times when it is inappropriate for it to be fun – the children may enjoy miming the prayer positions in Islam but your skill as a teacher will mean that you encourage them to do it with solemnity since to do otherwise would risk making a mockery of the act. Moreover RE often covers very serious topics – a discussion on death linked to the story of the crucifixion of Jesus is bound to be a sad one.

RE may not always be fun but it should be engaging and have the deeper pleasure that goes with true engagement. The children need to have their minds engaged by having lots of opportunities for thinking for themselves since thinking about what they are learning in terms of their own spiritual journey (AT2) is an essential part of RE. (See more in Chapter 5.)

You will need to engage the children's hearts if that journey is to be one worth taking. The affective dimension of RE is one that is especially emphasised in the 'Gift to the Child' material (Grimmitt et al., 1991, 2006) where the value of RE lies not in the accumulation of knowledge about religion but in it being an affective, transformative subject facilitating spiritual growth. Sue Philips' work on the Theatre of Learning also begins with and emphasises the affective by giving children experiences that are not explicitly religious – in Philips' terms they are religion-neutral – but they have parallels with religious experience. Such experiences include quiet reflection akin to meditation, the lighting of candles and the use of guided visualisation. (See more in the next chapter where principles are turned into practice.)

Wherever possible, plan to include physical activity in your RE lessons, not only to make the lessons more engaging but to reinforce and develop ideas. Drama, art, music-making and writing can provide the stimulus for discussion about abstract ideas and turn the abstract into something real and meaningful for the children.

Pedagogical principle 7: use as many senses as possible

Don't *talk* about food – give children the chance to *taste* it (observing health and safety issues) and if possible to cook it. A lesson on the Passover that includes tasting unleavened bread will be remembered longer than one with a picture of the bread, and one in which the bread is baked will be remembered for longer still. Use pictures and better still use real objects (see next chapter, Principles into practice) which children might touch. Burn incense sticks if you are teaching about Hindu puja, making sure you are not too near any asthmatic child, and smell spice boxes if you are teaching about the Jewish Sabbath.

A multisensory approach is important for all children but is especially important for children with learning difficulties or English as an additional language. Use of the senses not only motivates children but adds meaning and context to the words, making it much easier for them to understand. A child with severe language delay may not grasp the concepts underpinning a Hindu puja offering but they can smell the incense, feel the water on their skin and hear the bell. This relates to Standard Q19: *Know how to make effective personalised provision for those they teach, including those for whom English is an additional language or who have special educational needs or disabilities, and how to take practical account of diversity and promote equality and inclusion in their teaching*).

Conclusion

In reading this chapter you should have begun to think about and understand some of the issues and principles in teaching RE. It will be tempting when immersed in the day-to-day practice to forget some of these. Revisit them from time to time to remind yourself that teaching and learning are more complex and therefore more interesting than simply passing on information. We hope that the chapter has also given you ways to find a clear path through the subject.

A SUMMARY OF **KEY POINTS**

> **Religion can be described as having seven dimensions. These are all part of RE.**

> **Recognise your own understanding of religion and how it may affect your teaching.**

> **Being an atheist is not a bar to teaching RE well.**

> **There are facts and beliefs in the study of religion.**

> **Remember the child.**

> Start with the particular when teaching RE.
> Look for similarities between the religious phenomenon and the children's experience.
> Also acknowledge differences.
> Identify themes for learning from religions.
> Engage children's heads, hearts and hands.
> Use a multisensory approach where possible.

MOVING *ON* > > > > > > MOVING *ON* > > > > > > MOVING *ON*

Look at the next unit of RE you will be teaching. Apply these principles to your planning of that unit.

3
Principles into practice

Chapter objectives

By the end of this chapter you will have developed knowledge and understanding of:

- **teaching about festivals;**
- **skills in the use of resources in RE;**
- **skills of teaching strategies in RE;**
- **issues in taking children to visit a place of worship.**

This chapter addresses the following Standards for QTS: **Q17, Q22, Q25a,b, Q30**

Introduction

In the previous chapter we looked at some of the basic pedagogical principles in the teaching of RE. In this chapter we look at applying these principles to the study of religion and the resources available, though the narrative dimension is reserved until the next chapter.

The teaching strategies described below are ones that allow children to respond to, and work at their own level of attainment. In other words the differentiation is largely in the outcome. Children with learning difficulties, especially with language, will respond particularly to the use of the senses in RE though they may have more problems when asked to imagine them.

Festivals

For many children their first memorable encounters with their family's religion will be through the festivals. The majority of the children in this country of cultural Christian background first learn about it through Christmas and Easter, albeit in a commercialised and often secular form. Despite the clamour for presents and parties there are glimpses of religious content in the form of Father Christmas, who represents abundant giving, and some residue images of the baby in the cradle. All festivals are tangible, rich in taste, sight, sound and colour. They can be experienced from the youngest to the oldest even if the ideas expressed in them are not always understood. No wonder then that they are a popular entry point into the study of a religion.

Before we look at guidance for studying a festival, an issue and a word of warning. Many head teachers, in a bid for reverence for all faiths, like to announce that all the major festivals are celebrated in the school. Perhaps what they mean is that faiths are affirmed as worthy in the school, but there can be a problem in speaking of celebration of all festivals. In asking, indeed encouraging, children to celebrate all festivals you could be implying to them that they belong to all these religions.

The question centres on whether it is possible to celebrate something that is not one's own. We would argue that there are times when we celebrate something that is not strictly speaking ours. We may attend a wedding ceremony of someone of a faith not our own, but here we are celebrating the marriage not the faith. Christmas is often celebrated by people who are not Christians, perhaps because it is more than a religious festival but also a seasonal festival of mid-winter. Moreover, some communities, such as the Chinese community, actively invite people to participate in the fun of the festival; others though are more reticent since celebration of the festival is closely tied into identity. In both these examples there is some connection between those outside the faith and the festival.

We would suggest that there is a significant difference between being in a school with children from a faith community who might invite others to share their time of celebration, and being in a school where there are no members of that faith. For the latter to use the phrase 'celebrate the faith' verges on pretence and a lack of recognition of the importance of the festival for believers.

Moreover parents with strong religious convictions may well object to their children celebrating a festival not their own, since it could imply an invitation to a different belief. Muslims, Christians and Jews are the most likely to be concerned.

It is the word 'celebration' which is problematic. Studying the festival in an exciting and multisensory way is not. Indeed it is to be encouraged.

The word of warning is to do with planning. Festivals are a great starting point but a scheme of work that looked only at festivals would give a distorted picture of religious life and practice. Nevertheless, structuring a unit of work around a main festival can be a very positive way of approaching a new religion or revisiting a religion already familiar to them.

Here are some points to remember when studying a festival.

- Look at how the family prepares for the festival. Festivals don't just happen; they take days, perhaps weeks, of preparation. You can compare and contrast what happens in preparation for different festivals, e.g. a birthday party in a child's own home compared with the preparation for the festival. Younger children may help prepare a structured play area ready for the festival, e.g. spring cleaning the house ready for Passover.
- Some, but not all, festivals lend themselves very readily to a 'Gift to the Child' approach of introducing a powerful story for the children to encounter and engage with in its own right and then seeing that the story has such importance for some people they tell it each year at a major festival (see Chapter 4). Indeed the festival may include retelling the story through symbol and ritual, e.g. the story of the Flight from Egypt by the people of Israel is remembered each year at the Jewish festival of Passover and recalled in the foods and words of the Passover table.
- Festivals are very sensual experiences – they have smells, sounds, tastes, sights. It is always good practice to involve all the senses in RE, but never more so than in the study of festivals.
- Start with the particular. Describe the festival as it is practised by one family whether that family be one you've created or the family in a recording, that of a visitor, or indeed your own. Let the children tell you whether the festival is different and similar to their own celebrations.
- Festivals often contain powerful themes that can be developed into something for reflection or further investigation. Learn *from* religion as well as *about* it. For example, the festival of Passover, among other themes, is about freedom. It could well lead into finding out about the anti-slavery league and/or a class discussion with older children on whether a free person can do whatever they like, and if not why not?
- Festivals can be a good time to make connections between religions and science since most festivals are linked to the cycle of the year, e.g. What crops are sown or harvested at this time? A science topic on

light can be integrated with the study of those winter festivals that have a theme of light in them. Islam is the exception to the link with the cycle of the year since Muslims follow a lunar calendar, the new moon marking the beginning of the festival. What a good time for children to be noting the shape of the moon across the month, perhaps recording it every day, especially when Ramadan falls in the winter.

Some festivals are revisited every year in school as part of the ritual of the school year. Some of the whole-school rituals need to remain the same in that they provide a sense of continuity to the child, just as bringing out the same decorations for the Christmas tree provides continuity. However in the classroom there should be some development of understanding of the festival and with it personal understanding. You will need to make sure that you plan for progression and that the children are not just repeating what they have learnt at an earlier stage: *Plan for progression across the age and ability range for which they are trained, designing effective learning sequences within lessons and across series of lessons and demonstrating secure subject/curriculum knowledge (Q22).*

CASE STUDY

This inner city school has a majority of Muslim pupils. Therefore, Ramadan and Eid ul-Fitr are celebrated each year. The scheme of work builds in progression across the years. Each stage has a slightly different emphasis and in each stage the teacher would draw on what was happening at home.

- Foundation Stage: structured play area – Aysha's home. The emphasis is on one family celebrating the festival and the children talking about their experiences of the festival.
- Key Stage 1: The focus is on the prophet Muhammad and the revelation of the Qur'an which is celebrated in the last ten days of the month in particular. The planning, cooking and community aspects of the festival are emphasised.
- Lower Key Stage 2: The emphasis on the Revelation is taken a step further with a focus on the early Ummah, the Muslim community, and how the Qur'an was revealed, then copied by hand and then printed.
- Upper Key Stage 2: The focus is on giving – zakat. Children look into the work of Muslim charities and think about the idea of going without, self-discipline.

A final point to remember: don't say, though you will hear it often when studying a festival, *This is our Christmas,* or *Just like Christmas.* The celebration of festivals may have much in common, but there are also differences. For example, Muslim Ramadan and Eid are not tightly analogous to Christian Lent and Easter. Eid is a celebration of achievement, and ending. Yes, Ramadan is a time of self-discipline, but it is also one where the family are drawn closer together with many shared meals, often quite sumptuous. Many Muslims express genuine sorrow that the month has ended. On the other hand while Lent is also a period of self-discipline, the austerity lasts the whole time and is essentially a time that is about preparation for the major festival that lies ahead. The key items in common are that both are times of prayer and reflection with some discipline over food.

Using artefacts in RE

The use of religious artefacts can be a powerful means of engaging children with religion. A three-dimensional object that can be looked at from different angles, touched and sometimes even smelt is much more interesting than a flat photograph. Objects can give rise to awe, wonder and curiosity – the latter sometimes because of their aesthetic appeal, at other times because of their oddness.

The range of artefacts is enormous, from sacred texts, to prayer beads, to statues of Hindu gods, to play puppets. They can be obtained in gift shops, shops explicitly serving a religious community or through educational suppliers such as Articles of Faith.

Some artefacts need to be treated with great care and respect because of the value they hold within the faith, even if they are not expensive to buy. Out of respect for Muslim parents the Qur'an (Islam) or words from the Qur'an should not be on open view in a position lower than other texts in the room. Respecting the Qur'an in this way can also be a teaching point. The Qur'an should never be put on the floor or have anything placed on top of it. It should be wrapped in a clean cloth. The vast majority of Muslims will not touch the pages of the Qur'an without first washing ritually, and some may find it offensive for non-muslims to touch it. All these show the reverence and respect given to its words. However only the Qur'ans in Arabic require this level of respect. Translations of the Qur'an are regarded as translations not the holy book itself.

The holy books of the Torah (Judaism) and the Guru Granth Sahib (Sikhism) cannot be brought into the classroom except as facsimiles. Do not leave an image of the Guru Granth Sahib open on a flat surface where other items can be placed upon it as this may cause offence.

Other artefacts are less precious, though do be careful with anything that appears to have writing from a sacred text on it.

Some Muslim, Christian and Jewish children may not want to look at a Hindu statue of a god. It is thus much better to describe the object as a statue rather than a god. For many Hindus the statue does become the visible manifestation of the presence of God until it has been properly blessed but not before.

Think carefully about how you will introduce the artefact to the children – you will want to create an interest and curiosity and a sense of occasion. One delightful way of introducing a small artefact is to place it in an attractive cloth bag. You can then reveal it slowly to the children or let them feel it first. Another strategy is to set up a table either ready for the children or in front them so that they are beginning to ask 'What is this? What is it for?'. The table might be laid for Passover (Jewish) or look like a shrine.

With a large object give the children a lot of opportunity for really looking at it. One strategy is to follow this procedure.

1 Look closely at the object.
2 Now shut your eyes and draw it in your mind's eye (no touching of pencils yet).
3 Now look again to see what was missing.
4 Now draw it again in your mind's eye.
5 Now look again.
6 Now draw it.

The steps after the engagement will lead to different types of questioning or activities depending on the object. If it is a statue of the Buddha, encourage the children to comment on the mood and the hand gestures. What do they convey about the Buddha. If the object is a string of Muslim prayer beads you might count the number of beads. If you have laid a seder plate as if for Passover you might perform a small part of the ceremony. You may use the object as a stimulus for the children to do their own research.

At some point in the lesson you will need to put the object into its religious context. When is it used? How is it treated? If the artefact is the main focus for your lesson you will want to draw out a theme from it. For example, a discussion on the Hindu deity Shiva can lead to a discussion about change – what is negative about it, what is positive about it?

CASE STUDY

Year 1 were beginning a lesson on growing up in a Muslim family. Their teacher sat them in a circle in front of her and drew out a copy of the Qur'an contained in a zipped gold cover. She asked the children what they thought was inside the cover and why it needed a cover. She then very carefully opened the book to show the Qur'an inside, making sure that she didn't touch any of the pages. She demonstrated that the Qur'an opened from right to left, and she moved round the children showing them the pages – letting them note the different lettering. She then explained to the children that the book belonged to her friend Aysha, who is a Muslim and the book is very special to her because she is a Muslim. Aysha is going to mosque school to learn to read the Qur'an. She was thus putting the book in a context.

She then closed the book and put it on a high shelf to show respect. She asked the children to draw and write about an object which was special to them, thus linking the artefact to AT2 Learning from Religion but also helping the children make connections between Aysha's life and their own.

In the plenary the children talked about their own special object and the teacher reminded them of Aysha and the Qur'an.

The next RE lesson she told them a story that Aysha's mother had told her – how the Qur'an was revealed to Muhammad.

Other sorts of artefacts

Articles of Faith produce some toy versions of artefacts which can be used in play. These include an African bishop with a strong resemblance to Nobel Prize winner Archbishop Desmond Tutu, a soft model of a synagogue, and a doll which can reverse from being a ten-headed demon to the figure of the God Rama.

PRACTICAL TASK PRACTICAL TASK PRACTICAL TASK PRACTICAL TASK PRACTICAL TASK

Most schools have collections of religious artefacts. Make a list of those artefacts linked to the next unit of work you are teaching in RE and consider how you could use them effectively.

Using photographs in RE

Pictures of people engaged in religious ceremonies speak a thousand words. Pictorial Charts and Folens both produce a range of good photographs, and there are also many images on the World Wide Web, which can be printed or shown on a Smartboard. Families and friends can also be a useful source of photographs. A photo of yourself undergoing a ritual will be much more meaningful to the children than that of a stranger. Try to find a range of pictures that show the cultural diversity within a religion, for example the majority of Christians in the world are not white.

The first task is to help the children look closely at the picture, attending to its detail. There are a number of strategies for doing this, including the following.

- Children work in pairs – each pair has a different picture or you make multiple copies of the same picture. The children work back to back. One child describes the picture, the other child draws it. They then compare the drawing with the picture. If the children have had individual pictures their task is to describe it to other pairs in a group. This can then form the basis for the rest of the lesson.
- The children work in teams of four. One child is chosen to be the illustrator. Each child has a number. You call out the number 1s first who look at the image for 30 seconds and try to memorise it. They return to instruct the illustrator. You call out the number 2s and so forth. At the end of the activity you can ask them to reflect on how they have worked in teams before you go on to discuss the picture itself.
- Project a large complex picture onto a screen. The children write sentences describing the detail of things going on in the picture and then compare what they have seen and written with their neighbour.

Strategies that can follow a discussion of pictures include:

- asking the children to write thought and speech bubbles for the characters in the picture;
- the children working in groups to make a dramatic freeze frame of their picture and then unfreezing it to consider what happened next;
- alternatively children make up a cartoon strip showing the before and after scenes of their picture;
- asking the children to write a diary entry for someone in the picture.

> **PRACTICAL TASK** PRACTICAL TASK PRACTICAL TASK PRACTICAL TASK PRACTICAL TASK
>
> Find out what pictures are available in the school. Start your own collection of religious pictures. Write notes on sticky-notes on how they could be used. (Newspapers often have dramatic photos which provide interesting starting points for discussion.)

Using DVDs/video/TV programmes

DVDs, etc. fall into two main types. The first type is retelling of religious narratives (see the next chapter). The second type is programmes that introduce an aspect of the religion, usually a festival, through the eyes of a child. They often stress the ordinariness of the child concerned before looking at a family ritual the child observes because he or she is a member of a particular religion. Such programmes are thus excellent material for drawing out similarities and differences (see previous chapter). Remember that the children don't need to see the whole programme at once – a programme from *Water, Moon, Candle, Tree and Sword* (Channel 4) can be split so that the life of the child can be concentrated on in one lesson, and the story element viewed in the next. Clips from soap operas or the news can also be a useful resource if you are quick enough with the recorder. Lots of soaps have storylines featuring newborn babies, weddings and bereavement.

When planning you can build a whole lesson round the DVD as your starting point or use a clip to bring a point to life. You can link the DVD to artefacts by showing the children an artefact beforehand and then asking them to look out for it when watching the programme.

Afterwards ask older children to write down three things they remember from the clip and then share their list with a neighbour. Younger children can share one or two things they remember seeing with a talk partner.

Follow up questions and activities may include the following.

- How is the child's life similar to yours?
- What does he/she do because he belongs to the relevant faith?
- How does this fit in with what else we have learnt about this religion?
- A reflective activity associated with a theme.
- Follow up in other subject areas.

CASE STUDY

A Year 3 class viewed the programme 'Moon' on the *Water, Moon, Candle, Tree and Sword* DVD. After they discussed how their lives were like that of the boy in the DVD they noted the things he did because he was a Muslim. The children were particularly intrigued by everyone wearing white robes on pilgrimage. This led onto an important discussion of ways clothes show status and jobs. They were thus discussing a theme of equality, which is part of the pilgrimage. Follow up lessons included watching a story about Muhammad which picks up the theme of equality again, and a geography lesson on the location, climate and landscape of Saudi Arabia.

Visitors from the faith

The experience of meeting someone who is a practising member of the faith is extremely worthwhile if that someone is a person who can engage with children. The visitor need not be a member of the clergy – the best visitors are often parents, or someone who is a friend of yours or another teacher. The big advantage is that the religion becomes personal, particular and real. Encourage your visitor to talk about what they do as an individual rather than talk in general terms about the faith, e.g. how we observe Ramadan in our house, and to talk about feelings and recount anecdotes. Encourage them also to bring in artefacts and above all keep the time appropriate to the attention span of your children. If the person is a bit hesitant you can set it up as a question and answer session, e.g. *You were telling me about the time you . . .* Don't forget to check with the head teacher first and to be in the room at all times with the visitor. Visitors should NOT ask children to pray with them or do anything that may be construed as worship.

Guided visualisations

Guided visualisations can be a very calm peaceful way of helping children to use their imagination to conjure up ideas and places and of engaging them emotionally with the subject. They encourage the children to recall sensual information and perhaps apply it in a new context, in a type of mind drama. It is important to set ground rules first with the children, such as the importance of observing the silence and respect for others, and you should also consider whether you want to use music to add to the ambience. You then can take the children to the place by asking them to imagine. That place could be something known to them, such as a place they go to when they want to be on their own, or it could be somewhere requiring more imagination such as looking down on the earth from the moon. It might be a means of taking them back to the place of worship you have recently visited or you can guide them back through time to a place where the story you are about to tell them was first told. During the guided visualisation you can ask them to concentrate on the senses: What can you hear? What can you see above, below, to the right, to the left? What can you touch? What can you smell? The guided visualisation can then be a spring-board to discussion or activity.

CASE STUDY

Kelly, a Year 5 teacher, wanted to introduce her children to the idea of sacred sites. She asked the children to shut their eyes and breathe deeply before taking themselves in their minds to a place which was really important to them. She took them slowly through each of the senses so that they really imagined themselves in the place. She then asked them either to imagine themselves picking up something to remind themselves of the place or taking an imaginary photo of it. The children opened their eyes and drew their object before talking about it with their neighbour, including why the place was important to them. Kelly then used this as a platform for introducing the idea of places of pilgrimage.

Scripts for guided visualisations can be found from a number of sources, including Hammond et al. (1990).

The Theatre of Learning

The Theatre of Learning is an approach developed by Sue Phillips (2003), designed to engage children emotionally with the ideas and issues that mean they are learning from as well as learning about religion. It seeks to capture their heads, hearts and hands and is of value in itself as well as providing an entry point for understanding the relevant concepts. It can include activities that are religion-neutral parallels to explicitly religious activities, such as the following.

- Bake and share a cake to commemorate a favourite children's author. Put symbols of the author's work on the cake. Then look at a group of Christians meeting to share bread to remember Jesus.
- Fill an attractive bowl with water. Place floating candles on the surface. Give each child a piece of rice paper and a felt tip pen. Ask them to write about something they are sorry they did. Put them in the bowl and see them melt. Then use this as a way of introducing Jewish Day of Atonement and fasting for the day.
- Put out a small row of candles. As you light each one ask the children to think about (a) someone in need, (b) their own need, (c) somewhere in the world in need. Then ask them to think about how the experience was similar to and different from prayer. Look at some of the ways of praying within Buddhism – wheels, bells, flags. The children can write their wishes for others on flags and string them across the room.

Visiting a place of worship

Visiting a place of worship can be a very positive and exciting out-of-school experience for children if handled well (Q30). It can make the faith concerned come alive. The building may be the focus for a whole unit of work in studying a particular religion or it can be used as the opportunity to study similarities and differences as children compare and contrast two buildings within a religion or between religions.

The limits of the visit

As school visits will be during the week, it is likely that children will mainly see empty buildings. These may give clues to the use of the building and may prompt curiosity and awe and wonder but the children will miss the atmosphere of when it is in use. Brief visual recordings may complement the experience.

Remember too that most places of worship are not only used for worship but as places for community. Children may gather daily in the classrooms attached to the mosque to learn how to read the Qur'an; the communal meals held in the Sikh kitchen, the langar, are fundamental to the life and cohesion of the community.

The differences between faiths do not lie only in the choice of seating arrangements and decoration. For most religions with a regular weekly act of worship it is a time of common gatherings but in Chinese temples worship is much more of an individual or family affair, except at the times of festivals. And whereas congregations in Christianity are often largely made up of women, in Islam and Judaism it is the men who have a duty to go to mosque and synagogue, the women often saying their prayers at home.

For more on each faith see the Appendix page 131.

Preparation

You will need to prepare for the visit thoroughly.

- You will obviously need to carry out the same preparation as you would with any trip, i.e. seeking the permission of the head teacher, booking the bus if needed, carrying out a risk assessment.
- Permission from parents. You will need to emphasise in writing or talking to parents that this is an educational visit. The children will be learning about the building and the religion; they will not be worshipping.
- Discussion with the person showing you round. Some large places of worship such as cathedrals do have experienced educational staff who have a programme of different types of visit. Other popular places with regular school visits may have members of the community who especially deal with visitors. Often you will be shown round by a local leader or a member of the community. Whoever takes you round, it is always important to have a proper discussion to come to a mutual understanding about what you expect from the visit. It will be important to keep adult talk to a minimum, especially with young children.
- You are highly likely to visit the place when it is not being used for worship. Ask the relevant person

what sounds and smells would be part of an act of worship and see if some hint of these can be provided, e.g. via a recording or burning of an incense stick.

- Give the children guidance about the expectations on the visit. If you are visiting a mandir (Hindu), mosque (Islam) or gurdwara (Sikh) you and the children will be required to remove your shoes. Many children will take off their shoes as they enter their homes or those of friends so it won't feel strange to them. You can discuss why shoes are removed. Check with your host if you are uncertain. Better err on the side of modesty yourself rather than cause offence by seeming disrespectful.
- Be clear about your objectives: noting the furniture of the building may be important but perhaps more so is the opportunity for children to engage with the building and understand some of the activities which go on inside. The 'furniture' may give clues to the activities.
- Ask the children to note what they think they will see there. How much will of course depend to some extent on what specific teaching you have done about the faith beforehand.
- Make sure you have sketch books and/or digital cameras with you.
- If you are going to ask the children to write a guide book to the building ask them to identify what they will need to find out before they make the visit.

What to do when you get there? Here are some ideas.

- Give the children opportunities just to be in the place. Sit quietly with them and ask them to concentrate on sight, sound and smell. Build a quiet conversation with them about it, drawing out features of the worship from their observations.
- Ask the children to record features of the building which interest them with words and/or drawings and/or digital cameras. A viewfinder (i.e. cardboard frame) will help the children focus on one feature of the building. This can be followed up later in the classroom. The virtue of this approach is that it can encourage them to look closely as well as be quiet and concentrate. Ask the 'guide' to point out the features of the building which are important to him/her and then tell them what the place means to him/her. If a child in the class goes to the place for worship see whether they would like to be the guide.
- Ask the children to write down and then ask a question of the guide.
- Focus on a theme, e.g. Who is remembered in a church? Often lots of saints and local people, but also Jesus every Sunday in the celebration of communion.
- Look at the noticeboards. What else goes on in the building besides prayer and worship?

CASE STUDY

Tim, aged 6, decided to draw the wires emerging from the electricity box when on a visit to the local church. Back in the classroom the teacher asked him what the church needed electricity for. Tim was able to make the link to a microphone on the pulpit and suggested also lighting. His teacher showed him a picture of the candle sticks on the altar and discussed with him why they were there if they weren't used to provide light.

CASE STUDY

Mrs Taylor wanted to make the visit to the mosque memorable and meaningful for her Year 2 class so she told them the story of Abdul as they walked round the mosque. At each stop she told them what Abdul would do and asked the children to pretend they were Abdul. e.g. taking off his shoes, washing according to the ritual, standing in line on the marked carpet and imagining Mecca.

A word of warning – children very quickly note things and fasten onto things teachers and perhaps members of the faith would rather they didn't notice: the vacuum cleaner in the back of a prayer hall because the visit has disrupted the cleaning rota, a dirty sink, or shoes in a shambolic pile. This is why it is important for them to think about what the place looks like on the day of worship.

Follow up to visits

Back in the classroom children need to make sense of, consolidate and extend the experiences and learning they have had on the visit. The starting point, and perhaps the most important part of all, is the opportunity for them to talk about the visit. How did it make them feel? What surprised them? What did they feel they learnt about the beliefs of the people who went there regularly? What did they learn about their ideas about God?

You may not always be able to reply with a satisfactory answer. Children may well feel puzzled and perhaps cross with the fact that men and women worship separately in the place, and the carpets for the women are shabbier. You can wonder with them what a person of the faith might say (perhaps the women are cross about it themselves or perhaps they are glad because it's easier when looking after babies).

Other activities
- Discussions and research built on the sketches children have made. What is the item? What is its significance?
- Children prepare a guide book to the building based on the information they have gained. This might also link with history and geography.
- Children look at their own classroom and plan the alterations they would need to make to turn it into the relevant place of worship.
- Children compare one or two pictures of exteriors of other places of worship of the faith either from hardcopies or with images on the world wide web. What do they have in common; what is different?
- Children make an interior 'dolls' house' model of the place of worship in a small cardboard box.
- Children listen to some of the sounds that take place in the building with their eyes closed and imagining they are sitting in the building.
- Listen further to extracts of music associated with the place of worship.
- Turn a structured play area into a church, mosque, etc. for a short period.
- Find out about wedding ceremonies in the faith. Children draw or make a model of their particular building decorated ready for a wedding and put the bride and groom in the middle. (Remember though that not all religions have the wedding ceremonies in the place of worship.)
- Children make a simple hypertext guide to their local place of worship to place on the school Website.

ICT

The internet can be a wonderful source of images and short video clips for use on your interactive whiteboard if you are prepared to trawl through what appears on Google and use them discerningly. For example, a Website of Auburn Gallipoli mosque has a very short clip showing a man calling Muslims to prayer from the top of a minaret – great for bringing it to life. The Espresso package has some excellent short introductory clips on religion which can be incorporated into your lesson plans. However by far the best resource is www. reonline. org. uk which discusses resources and issues and also gives you links to other sites, including primary schools who have used ICT effectively in RE. ICT of course can be used as a means of making products that draw on research in the subject (see Chapter 5).

Conclusion

There are many interesting and exciting ways you can study religion in the classroom so that the experience is engaging and meaningful to the children. These are just a beginning. The personnel as well as the store cupboard at school are wonderful resources, as are places in your local area including places of worship. Furthermore, it is worth making a trip to a place of worship not available locally so that you can bring the religion alive to children. Do make use of the opportunities around you.

A SUMMARY OF **KEY POINTS**

> **Similarity and difference are important concepts in learning about festivals, artefacts and places of worship.**

> **Respect for religious sensibilities is important in learning about festivals, artefacts and places of worship.**

> **There are opportunities for learning from religions in the study of festivals, artefacts and places of worship.**

> **Be imaginative in your use of resources and your approach to teaching RE.**

> **The internet contains useful resources for RE.**

MOVING *ON* > > > > > > MOVING *ON* > > > > > > MOVING *ON*

Visit a local place of worship and make contact with the leader there. Plan a visit with the children in the class and then build your follow up activities on the things which interest them.

Or, look at your local area for evidence of the impact of belief and culture. Look at the high street as well as places of worship.

4
Literature, literacy and RE

Chapter objectives

By the end of this chapter you will have developed knowledge and understanding of:

- **the role of stories in RE;**
- **strategies for using stories in RE lessons;**
- **the confident use of stories in RE;**
- **issues surrounding religious literacy.**

Standards addressed in this chapter: **Q14, Q23, Q25**

Introduction

When you open up your Local Agreed Syllabus, or look at your school's Scheme of Work for RE, you will no doubt see listed some stories, or at the very least religious texts that contain stories. The level descriptors for RE in the QCA Non-Statutory Guidelines (2004) for Religious Education Key Stages 1 and 2 refer to recounting and retelling stories (AT1 levels 1 and 2) and at levels 3 and 4, how religious ideas are expressed in stories.

Some of the stories you may be called upon to tell will be linked to the festivals of the religions you will be covering, and to the lives of the key figures in the faith. For example – the story of the death and resurrection of Jesus found in the New Testament is at the heart of an understanding of the Christian festival of Easter, the escape from Egypt is integral to an understanding of the Jewish festival of Passover, and Hindu festivals recall the Ramayana.

You may be delighted at the prospect of this story-telling – you like stories yourself and you recall with pleasure listening to stories, including religious stories, in school. On the other hand you may recoil at the memory of being bored, as teachers read you dry versions of the tales in a dry voice.

You may have a problem with the word 'story' itself since it conjures a notion of the fable, or a novel, something that is untrue. It may be important for you because you are a believer in a particular faith, with a particular stance, that the stories of the faith found in its scriptures are literally true and therefore you want to call them history. Or else you may feel some concern because you feel you are expected to teach stories you don't believe in as though they were true.

Here, we use 'story' as a generic term to include any recount or narrative text. It will be used for stories that may be historical, e.g. the story of Gandhi, or for those that make no claim to be history, e.g. parables. One of the challenges in RE is that there are many stories which some believers regard as literally true, some believers regard as basically symbolic and those outside the faith may dismiss entirely. The story of Creation found in Genesis 1, a book belonging both to the Jewish holy book the Torah and the Christian holy book the Old Testament, is an example of such a story.

This chapter addresses some of these issues and aims to alleviate some of those fears by developing an approach to the teaching of stories in RE.

PRACTICAL TASK PRACTICAL TASK PRACTICAL TASK PRACTICAL TASK PRACTICAL TASK

Look at the Local Agreed Syllabus for your local authority or the appropriate religious syllabus if you are in a faith school. Which religious stories are listed? Which ones do you know already? Which ones, if any, do you feel comfortable telling? Why tell religious stories? The first answer is, of course, because they are in the syllabus. They are there primarily because they are part and parcel of developing knowledge and understanding of the relevant faith (Attainment Target 1, QCA, 2004).

However, if you see and appreciate their value for children's development and capacity to participate in discussions about questions of meaning you will be more ready and able to use them in the advance of Attainment Target 2, Learning from Religion (QCA, 2004).

There are three main reasons for telling stories from religions. First, these stories may have intrinsic value for children's development because they deal with universal themes of being human, in relationship with the world including other humans. Their distance from the here and now may be their strength – there is space in the story for children to home in on the similarity to their own lives. They may recognise themselves or their family in the story; the story may help them deal with feelings and emotions. Grimmitt et al. (1991) developed this in their *A Gift to the Child* pack (2006), where the stories are chosen because of what they can offer to the child in terms of powerful themes. Jonah, for example, may be a story of a crusty, cantankerous man who runs away from God's command and is swallowed by a whale yet children are drawn to it – partly because of the very idea of being swallowed by a whale, but also perhaps because of the psychological drama of disobedience and repentance.

Secondly, the value of the story for the child may not be immediate but may come into its own at a later date when familiarity with the story allows the adult to engage with other images and stories dealing with religious themes. There are many stories which, although not children's stories, are unlikely to be met in adulthood unless one belongs to a religious faith; yet once acquired they provide a valuable pool of extended metaphors with which to interpret experience.

Furthermore all areas of enquiry have their own language and manner of discourse – to be scientifically literate includes knowing the vocabulary of science and how scientific debate is organised around hypotheses. To be religiously literate a person needs familiarity with the stories which are the reference points for discussion and which fill out the concepts within and across faiths. For example, a discussion of the concept of sacrifice may be built on children's experiences of personal or heroic sacrifice, but a richer understanding requires recognition of the sacrifice in different faiths from the death of Jesus in the Christian story to the Buddhist Atoka tales of early incarnations of the Buddha – such as the Monkey King who offers himself as a bridge to allow his followers to escape the assault of men.

A third reason for telling stories from religions to children is to help them learn to interpret such stories with reference to the texts and to their own experience and knowledge of the world. You are teaching them to be interpreters. If you are teaching in a religious school it may be your duty to teach children to interpret according to the interpretative tradition of the religion concerned. In a community school, a major reason for telling religious stories is to help children develop the ability to make informed choices about religion, which includes how they respond to religious stories. Education is, after all, about helping children think for themselves. As educators we want them to be open to learning from texts, including narratives, but not be subservient to them. This applies to all texts, oral and written, including religious ones. Hollindale (1992) in his *Ideology and the Children's Book* writes of the importance of freeing children from being at the mercy of what they read (or hear). This applies as much to stories from religion as anything else.

An important component of learning to interpret texts is awakening children to the possibility of thematic and metaphorical interpretations of texts. Most primary children will interpret stories in a concrete way, with Key Stage 2 children being especially interested in whether a story 'really happened'. Nevertheless you as the teacher can ask questions that encourage children to think about why the story is told and what it makes them think about.

Classroom practice

Let's now think in more detail about the practicalities of teaching these stories. Your lesson plan will obviously begin with a learning objective.

Your learning objective for using a story in class will always be the same:

- to enable the children to become familiar with, engage with and interpret religious stories; and sometimes you will add a second specific learning objective as follows;
- for children to recognise that [title of story] is of special importance to people who follow this 'religion' and may be told in a special context.

Your expectations for the quality of interpretation will depend on the level of emotional and literary development of the children in the class.

But you will also have a rationale, whether recorded or in your head, as to why you have chosen this story. If you are required to tell the story by the scheme of work then think through for yourself as to why it is included.

What about the moral of the story?

It may be tempting to think to yourself 'This is a religious story. Therefore it must have a moral; therefore I must identify the moral to make sure that the children understand it. My objective is to ensure that children understand the meaning of the text.' Such thinking is to misunderstand religious stories.

While many religious stories were told originally for didactic purposes about morality, many were not. The parables of Jesus, for example, according to some theologians, were told primarily to announce God's coming kingdom rather than to give a specific moral message. Some religious stories are even morally dubious, such as Hindu stories about the boyhood pranks of Krishna, or the Biblical story where Jacob tricks his father into giving him the birthright instead of his brother.

Moreover there is a very big question as to whether children can understand adult inter-pretations of the texts. They may be wonderful at forming their own metaphors but they have difficulty in following the metaphorical meaning of others. Indeed Ronald Goldman (1964) in a highly influential study, after studying children's understanding of Bible stories regularly told in school, concluded that children generally were unable to comprehend the meaning he believed that texts held. His findings have largely been upheld, though the growth in multifaith RE is one reason why his further conclusion that, with rare exception, children should not be told Bible stories has been set aside by syllabus writers.

One modern literary theory offers an answer to three basic issues:

1 Is this story true or not?
2 What meaning of the text am I trying to teach?
3 Can a child understand an adult text?

This theory, known as the 'transactional theory of interpretation' (Cainey, 1990), suggests that there is always more than one meaning to a narrative text. The meaning is made in the interaction between the text and the life experiences and concerns of the reader.

We can see this very clearly in the history of interpretation of religious texts where for example, feminist readings of a Biblical story, while still paying close attention to texts, will create a different reading than that of a conservative male theologian. Although attempts may be made to recover the author's original intent, the meaning is always more than the author intended, and furthermore, where an oral tradition lies behind a story, it is almost impossible to get back to the original story.

Concerns that children will interpret the text differently to adults dissolve with this approach. Of course the children's readings will be just that, children's readings and not adults'. Over the years they will mature in their interpretations of the stories. As children grow teachers will have an important role in helping them to move away from literal and literalistic mean-ings, and open them up to other ways of understanding and/or of finding truth claims in the texts. Thus it is not your job to help the children to find a specific moral to a story, to tell them whether it is true or not, or to lead them to the right meaning. Instead, your role is to help the children acquire the skills to become critical readers/interpreters who engage with the text, pay attention to the detail, justify their views and listen to the views of others. You can also provide them with some historical context where appropriate, and you can help them understand that the story may have particular significance within a community. In the light of this it is vital that children re-visit stories as they mature in order to build on and extend their earlier understanding.

Choosing the story

Your choice of story will usually be linked to Agreed Syllabus requirements and schemes of work.

Planning the lesson

In planning your use of stories in the classroom you will need to consider:

- how to help children become familiar with the story and engage with it;

- how to interpret the story;
- put the story in the context of its religion of origin.

Sometimes your work on a story will last just one lesson, so you will cover all three steps simply in one lesson. With a more complex story, especially an epic one, the process may take several sessions.

Becoming familiar with and engaging with a story

You will need to consider the choice of version of the story. Will you read it, if it is a Biblical story, from a translation of the original text such as the Good News Bible or the New International Version? This has the advantage of bringing the children as close to the original story as possible and is recommended by writers such as the Gobbles (1986), who argue that children should have a direct access to the text. However, this has the disadvantage in that many Bible stories are told very sparingly, without opportunity to build up an atmosphere, and for the listener to assimilate what is happening. Furthermore the language may be alienating for a first listening. The King James translation from the early seventeenth century can be read as part of school worship, especially at Christmas, to stir a sense of mystery and wonder and enable children to become familiar with the cadences of the poetry, but telling the story in your own words or using a modern version will make it more accessible to the children

Besides which, the majority of religious stories outside the Judaeo-Christian tradition are not found in definitive versions. Stories about Muhammad, for example, are found in collections called Hadith. The Qur'an, the sacred text of Islam, refers to stories, rather than telling them directly. Likewise the stories of the Sikh gurus are not part of the sacred literature.

Your choice is to tell the story in your own words or to find a well-told version. Telling in your own words can be a bit daunting, but is worth the time and trouble. You need to practise it, in your head at least, beforehand so that you are comfortable with it. It is perhaps the best way of holding an audience because it gives you the freedom to be dramatic.

When looking for a written version, you should consider the complexity of the language rather than the specific vocabulary. Younger children will need a more simple sentence and repetition than older children. Well-told stories often have a sense of rhythm and pace to them. You should also choose a telling of the tale that reflects the tone of the original, at least for the first telling. For example, jokey, frivolous versions of the Noah story distract from the power of a story of judgement and salvation.

There are also some good video retellings such as the BBC series for older children *Testament*, and the *Monkey King and other tales*, Buddhist stories produced by the Clear Vision Trust.

Getting started – telling the story

The authors of *A Gift to the Child* (Grimmitt et al., 1991) recommend an 'entering device'. The children sit in a circle and a candle is lit, or a bell rung to signal entering into a sacred space. We are a little dubious of this, in that we think it is important not to draw too firm a boundary between religious and secular stories. Such tactics may also discourage children from questioning the story.

It is important to capture the children's attention and convey to them that this story is worth hearing. You can do this through using an artefact, central to the story, setting up a mystery, or simply, and probably mainly, through your tone of voice. Sometimes you will launch straight into a story, at other times you may decide to do something more deliberate such as taking children on an imaginary journey back through time, or playing a piece of mood-setting music.

Give the children time to think and ponder, especially if the story is a moving one. If the story is a long one leave it on a cliff-hanger until the next time.

Remembering the stories

Have the names of key characters written on the board – the names may be unfamiliar so may need repeating. If telling in your own words, describe the scene and ask the children to shut their eyes and imagine it.

Closed questions focusing on plot detail can kill a story. Instead, if the story is a short one, read it again, or the simplest, quickest method, if it is longer, is to ask the children to shut their eyes and imagine various scenes.

Rewriting the story in their own words may also have a deadening effect. Instead:

- ask the children to a draw a quick cartoon strip of the key scenes in the story and then compare their choice with that of a neighbour;
- ask them to draw one or two scenes and then place them in chronological order with those of other children in their group;
- have a collection of objects or picture of an object and ask the children to help you put them in the right order, for example, if you have told the story of the four sights of the Buddha show children a medicine bottle, a walking stick, a picture of a coffin and a monk's begging bowl.

Here are some further strategies for helping children engage with the stories.

- Divide the children into groups to discuss the feelings of a particular character in the story. Hot-seat that character, perhaps pretending you are a time travelling reporter, or have children in that role.
- Ask the children to freeze-frame scenes. Touch a child lightly on the shoulder indicating you want him or her to unfreeze and talk about what the character is feeling.
- Ask the children to draw a scene and to put the thoughts of the characters in thought bubbles.
- Ask the children to write a letter home as though they were one of the characters in the story.
- Do an emotions graph of the story by tracking the feelings of the different characters. Put the key points of the story on the horizontal line. If the character is feeling positive at that point in the story, his/her symbol is put at an appropriate position above the line. If the character is negative the symbol is put below the line. Help the children find the most apposite word to describe the emotion.
- Ask the children to write a newspaper report about the events.
- Ask the children to prepare a short tune to accompany each of the main characters, or the mood music for a retelling of the story.
- Ask the children to retell the story in a different setting, for example, the Christian story of the Good Samaritan really lends itself to this.

All these strategies will help children to develop their literacy skills: *Design opportunities for learners to develop their literacy, numeric and ICT skills* (Q23).

Don't forget to revisit the stories, by telling them again. Children love to hear stories again and again, and as long as you do it in an interested manner, it is a good way of helping them absorb it. However, if you are revisiting a story from an earlier year make sure you give them the opportunity to think about it again and gain new insights. By the time they are in Year 6 children can be comparing different Biblical accounts of the birth story of Jesus rather than being confined to infant versions.

Interpreting the story

Careful, open questioning is the key to this. The following questions are useful starting points for discussion.

- How did the story make you feel?
- What do you think of the story?
- Why do you think a character behaved in a certain way?
- What do you think of the way he/she behaved?
- What do you think the story is trying to teach?
- Why do you think (Jesus/Muhammad) told this story?
- What does this story tell us about (Jesus/Muhammad/Moses/Guru Nanak, etc.)?
- Does the story remind you of another story that you know? In what way?
- Why do they think a parent of the faith would tell it to their children?

Sometimes you may wish to expand the horizons of the story by helping the children think about characters forgotten by the text, e.g. I wonder what Peter's wife felt when he stopped being a fisherman to follow Jesus?

Follow through children's answers by listening carefully and asking gentle follow-on questions, e.g. What bit of the story made you think that? Ask others in the class whether they agree or disagree? Unless the children are working in pairs it is often best to have children seated in circles for such discussions and to remind them of the basic rules of considerate listening.

Do NOT offer children your interpretations or solutions to any problems they raise. Instead return them to the story or to the views of others (see chapter 5 on Community of enquiry). For example, if they ask you whether Noah's flood was like a tsunami, then help them make a comparison between the flood in the story and a major flood today.

Comparison of versions or interpretations is often a useful strategy.

- Compare two different versions of the story. How are they similar and different? What are the different authors and artists trying to emphasise? This links closely with the literacy strategy. Look at the illustrations as well as the words.

- Look at a painting of a scene from the story or compare two artists' paintings. The Christmas story especially lends itself to this activity because it has been painted so many times, but you can also find different illustrations of Hindu myths and legends. Decode paintings with the children. Such strategies can help children think through the artist's interpretations of the subject, and help alert children to different interpretations.

Putting the story in a context

A good story is universal; it transcends the boundaries of the religion or tradition from which it springs. Nevertheless, if one point of telling the story is to build up knowledge and under-standing of a particular faith then children need to know its context. Some tactics are:

- to link the story with a child or family of the religion you have introduced earlier: for instance, the story of Muhammad's call could be linked to a mother telling her child the most important story of the Muslim religion;
- to link the story with a festival, e.g. the telling of the Biblical story of the jewish flight from Egypt would be followed by looking at how the Passover meal remembers the story; the story of Holy Week can be directly linked with Easter; in both cases the festivals retell the story in word, symbol, and song;
- to say simply that the story comes from a particular religious text.

Contextualisation can happen before or after the telling of the story. Don't let it get in the way of the children engaging with the story. Putting in context is also vital because it is a process of distancing the child from the story. It is a recognition that however universal the story is in its themes, the explicit beliefs may be those of a particular community which the child does not necessarily share. (See the introduction to Volume One of *A Gift to the Child*, Grimmitt et al., 1991).

Planning for developing speaking and listening skills

Speaking and listening are clearly essential to the use of a story. Short, snappy stories will still have a place with older children, but on the whole you will extend the listening time and the complexity of the story to develop listening skills as you would with your reading of fiction.

Learning to express their own ideas about the story and listen respectfully to the views of others is also essential. Encourage the children to follow on what another child has said, by asking whether someone has something to add.

Some of the best conversations will occur when the children are drawing or doing another such activity. Here they will be in small groups and may feel more confident to speak, especially if you prompt them with a thoughtful question.

But what if. . .

The question from a child which many teachers fear with regard to stories in RE is the one that asks 'Is this true?' The response can be 'What do you think?' followed by a 'Why?' or one that recognises the diversity of answers 'Well, I don't know, some people believe it really happened but I don't agree', and if you think it is a good story you might add, 'But I still think it's a great story because people often behave like that, don't they?'

You may also wish to respond from your own religious perspective, 'As a Christian I believe...' If you have the confidence do explore with children how stories may be of value, reflecting real emotions without necessarily being literally true. The information box at the end of the chapter may help you think about the ways that stories may contain valuable truths and ideas without being literally true.

> ### REFLECTIVE TASK
>
> Re-read a story from religion you were told as a child. Ask yourself why it was told in the first place and consider how your understanding of it has changed. Ask yourself whether you are stuck with a literalistic interpretation and then try to identify the themes and issues you experience in it as an adult.

Some doubts

Although we are of the view that there are a multitude of religious stories which will engage children if told well, there are some stories we feel are best left to secondary school, when the children may have the maturity to deal with the difficult issues therein. One such story is found in the QCA Units of study for RE. Unit 3E recommends telling the story of Abraham's act of faith in being willing to sacrifice his son, Isaac. This is a story in which God asks Abraham to commit a fundamentally immoral task – that of human sacrifice. Sometimes teachers tell the Islamic version of the story because it is associated with the festival of Eid ul-Adha.

One interpretation of the story is that is was told to demonstrate that God does not require human sacrifice, because in the end a lamb or goat is offered instead. However, the story, as it is told, does not question the right of God to ask for human sacrifice and within our twenty-first century moral outlook amounts to child abuse.

It is a powerful story, one that raises many important issues, and one that is found in the three faiths of Judaism, Christianity and Islam. However, in our view the vast majority of primary school children will not have the critical thinking or emotional maturity to cope with it. It could do great damage unless the teacher has the courage to challenge it at this stage. The QCA documents are not legally mandatory.

Exploring religious literature

Secular stories

One consequence of Goldman's work in the 1970s and 1980s was the promotion of children's literature that implicitly explored religious ideas. Reading and discussing such stories was seen as central to RE. It was recognised that children's literature was of value at the current stage of children's development, but could also prepare them for comprehending central Biblical themes. Perhaps the most popular story of all was *Dogger* by Shirley Hughes (1977), in which a girl, Bella, swaps a new teddy, just won at a fair, for the battered old plush dog lost by her younger brother, but bought by a small girl from a stall. This act of generosity and kindness is held up as a good example to the children and also precurses the idea of sacrifice, central to a number of faiths. Other children's books offer ways of thinking about themes such as death (e.g. *Badger's Parting Gifts*, Varley, 1984), separation and reconciliation (*Where the Wild things Are*, Sendak, 1967) and identity (*I am David* by Ann Holm, 1989, recounting the tale of a Jewish child finding his identity after the Holocaust).

In the 1970s and 1980s reading such books was seen as RE overlapping with English. The demarcation of subjects into discrete curriculum areas and, following the 1988 and 1992 Education Acts, the rise of explicit teaching about religious belief and practice has led to such literature being shifted out of the domain of RE. Teachers with a deep understanding of text level work in English and/or with a passion for children's literature have continued to read such books in a manner that helps children explore themes within them. It doesn't matter whether such activities are named as RE or English education, so long as children have the benefit of engaging with such texts and exploring the themes in an open manner. Nevertheless, any breaking down of boundaries between subjects so that teachers see the value for both RE and literature in reading such books (and more traditional religious texts) is to be welcomed. See information box below and the Bibliography for recommended books.

> **PRACTICAL TASK** PRACTICAL TASK **PRACTICAL TASK** PRACTICAL TASK **PRACTICAL TASK**
>
> Read a children's picture book and a book for older children What human experience themes do they contain? Why might they be of value to children's religious/spiritual development? What links might be drawn to religious concepts that you are familiar with?

Further words on religious literacy

Any domain of enquiry has its own vocabulary and own way of using vocabulary. As we have seen already, both religious and secular stories help develop concepts such as sacrifice, mystery and redemption, though at primary school stage the specific vocabulary may not be used.

There is a place though for developing an understanding of some of mysterious words of religion, and thus some religious literacy outside the world of stories. 'Prayer', for example, is a word associated with the religious life but it may be alien to many children, so they will have little insight into what it can mean to religious people. It is here that bridges can be built between the conceptual world of the child and religious worlds (Cooling, 2000). Thus on the subject of prayer, the starting point may be discussions of times of feeling thankful, or hoping someone would recover from an illness. Much of religious language and literacy depends on the capacity to play with words, making analogies, similes and metaphors that all work in this area also provides a foundation for RE. For example, similes may be a useful starting place for exploring perhaps the most difficult concept of all, 'God'.

A lesson exploring ideas about God could begin with the children ending sentences using abstract concepts:

> Happiness is like a feather because . . .
> Happiness is like a book because . . .
> Happiness is like a river because . . .

The children could then go on to make their own similes about God. Such a lesson would enable children to give voice to their ideas and listen to one another in a non-threatening, open way. Because these are open-ended activities children can join in whatever their level of attainment, even though they are abstract ideas.

A poetic approach can also be employed when exploring the poems of faith from the Psalms in the Old Testament (Tenach) to the hymns of the Sikh Guru Nanak.

Non-narrative texts

Much of religious scripture is not narrative. It is important that some of this material is made accessible to children, so that they begin to know what is inside the scriptures rather than simply treating them as artefacts. The Sikh scriptures, for example, are a collection of hymns, many of them about the wonders of nature. Verses can be examined as poetry. Similarly some of the Biblical psalms, a hymn book of Jew and Christian can be read as poetry by children. Psalm 23, 'The Lord is my shepherd', being one whose imagery is readily available to upper junior children. Children may want to take it a step further and explore other metaphors for God which spring from several faiths, e.g. 'The Lord is my comforter', or 'The Lord is my judge'.

As with story, the objective of the lesson is to make a meaning, but here the emphasis would be on exploration of the imagery. Asking children to illustrate the poem with borders with appropriate imagery after copying out a section of a passage is one way of doing this. Making up one's own poem on a similar theme is another method of engagement and interpretation.

Other genres of religious texts can be used in a symbiotic relation with literacy. If it is a literacy lesson the objectives will be literacy, but the text will be reinforcing or extending knowledge and understanding gained in the RE lesson. For example, a visit to the mosque and discussion on prayer might be followed by looking at an instruction manual for wudu ritual washing. Conversely the primary objectives could be RE but this might be coupled with a reiteration of a literacy lesson on instructions.

Some examples of non-fiction texts that are readily available are:

- rules from the Qur'an, the Torah and the New Testament;
- proverbs and other wise sayings;
- advertising leaflets about forthcoming events or charities;
- recipes for foods associated with festivals;
- newspaper items;
- parish magazines.

Case studies

The following case studies examine the role of the teacher as facilitator of discussion in the context of a story.

CASE STUDY 1:
HANDLING THE QUESTION OF WHETHER A STORY IS TRUE OR NOT AND ENCOURAGING THINKING ABOUT A STORY

Anna told her Year 2 class the story of the revelation of the Qur'an as part of a unit of work on growing up in a Muslim family. In the previous lesson using photographs (she might equally have used a doll), she introduced the children to a Muslim child she called Aysha, creating a story about her life. The lesson focused on Aysha going to mosque school to learn to read the Qur'an.

In lesson two Anna showed the children the Qur'an again, taking it down from a high place in the classroom, and unwrapping it, thus demonstrating it is a precious book. She told the children that they were going to hear the very special story that Aysha's

---

mother tells her about how the Qur'an came into being. Anna has thus given them a context for the story. She asked the children to shut their eyes and imagine the cave of Hira, far away in a hot dry country, and then the she told them the story of the revelation to Muhammad.

She knew that, out of respect for Muslim sensibilities, she couldn't ask the children to draw Muhammad so instead she asked them to think about the feelings and colours of each stage of the story as she recapped the tale and allowed it to sink in. Next, she allowed the children to give their own responses. Tim enthused about angels, telling his own story of an angel. Freya, more of a sceptic, asked, 'Did that really happen?' Anna was stumped at first; she knew that Muslims believe this is a historical event that happened on a particular day and year, but she was not a Muslim. 'What do you think?' she asked Freya. 'It's got an angel. I don't think there really are angels. But you said it happened in Saudi Arabia and that is a real country. Is it true?' came the answer.

Anna replied that, yes, Freya was right, Saudi Arabia is a real country and that Aysha's family believe that this is what really happened, as do other people who are Muslims. But Freya asked again. 'What do *you* think?' This time Anna replied, 'No, I don't think I share that belief, but I think something special must have happened to Muhammad, because it inspired him to start telling people to worship one God rather then many gods.'

Anna rounded off the lesson by returning to Aysha. She asked the children to think about why Aysha's family told the story. Time was up, but she could have followed the lesson through with the children designing a cover for a Qur'an, or by drawing their own special book.

In the next lesson the children looked at the month of Ramadan, which includes much study of the Holy Book and a celebration of the revelation on the Night of Power. Anna had introduced the children to a central story in Islam and also made space for them to respond to the story in their own way.

CASE STUDY 2:
THINKING ABOUT STORIES SYMBOLICALLY – THE RAMAYANA WITH A YEAR 5 CLASS

Tim was a PGCE final placement student taking a Year 5 class. It was nearly Diwali. He knew that the children had heard the Ramayana several times before in a children's version. He wanted to do something different and he wanted the class to think about the story in more depth. He gave the children each a sheet of paper with a thought bubble on it. He asked them to draw Sita sitting in the magic circle, and then put her thoughts in the bubble. He was pleased with the response. Lots of children wrote about Sita feeling safe, but a couple suggested Sita's annoyance at being treated like a child, and not being able to go hunting with the men. He then asked them to think about what would have happened if Sita had not disobeyed Rama, by helping the holy man. In the next lesson they looked at the life of Gandhi who died with a prayer to Rama on his lips. They discussed what 'evil' Gandhi was fighting and the tools he used to fight it. The children then discussed in groups the problems of fighting violence with violence.

Later the children made a ten-headed monster and put 'evils' on the heads that they could 'fight' in their own way. One child suggested 'global warming' another 'child abuse' another 'jealousy' and another 'swearing'. The children then worked in pairs to list suggestions on how they could 'fight' these.

In allowing questioning and in encouraging children to think about the story in a symbolic way Tim was opening up the possibility of non-literalistic readings of the story.

CASE STUDY 3:
ENCOURAGING CHILDREN TO MAKE LINKS TO THEIR OWN LIVES

Mrs Edwards, in a suburban community school, told the story of the twins Jacob and Esau from the Biblical book of Genesis to a Year 3 class. She described Esau as the hairy one, his father's favourite, and Jacob as the one who liked to be at home with his mother and do the cooking. A look of recognition passed over the face of John. Mrs Edwards paused, 'Yes, John.' 'That is like me, I like being in the kitchen with my mother,' a response that was unpredictable and yet valuable. The child had been given a story which helped him affirm his identity.

CASE STUDY 4:
STORIES CAN RAISE QUESTIONS OF MEANING

Glenda told her Year 3 class the Hindu story behind how the god Ganesh got his elephant head. She had been worried the children would be upset by the violence in the story, which involves the beheading of a boy whose head is then replaced with an elephant's head, but wanted to look at the story because Ganesh is such a popular god in Hinduism. To her surprise the children were firstly concerned about the welfare of the elephant, and secondly a few became embroiled in a long discussion on whether Ganesh was boy or elephant. The story had initiated a discussion on identity. This was possible because Glenda encouraged open discussion which meant the children raised the questions they were interested in.

CASE STUDY 5:
DEALING WITH PREJUDICES WITHIN THE STORY

Melanie was telling her mainly Muslim class the story of the Good Samaritan. She was aware that the story can come across as very anti-Semitic, because it talks about the Jews as the passers-by who neglect the man who has been robbed. She recognised that the children were not quite ready to grasp the full significance that both Jesus and his audience were Jewish and that the point of the story was that the Jews and the Samaritans were enemies. She decided to tell the story from the point of view of the victim and instead of saying Jewish she said, 'He saw a priest from his own tribe'. Later, she asked the children to make up a modern version of the story, asking the children to consider two groups of people who were 'enemies'. Taking the characters from two opposing football teams was a popular response.

Here Melanie has maintained the spirit of the story but avoided a telling which might reinforce the children's own prejudices.

Genres of religious stories
(a) Myths
The word myth is difficult to define: however, grand-scale stories about the ways of God or Gods which do not have a historical context are usually regarded as myth. The story either transcends history or belongs to pre-history, before the world was as it is now. Thus many myths are to do with creation: how the world was created; how human beings were created; where suffering comes from; how fire was created. They were told in the first place to explore these existential and natural questions and they reflect deep beliefs held about them.

One feature of myths is that they were part of a long oral tradition before they were finally written down, e.g. many of the stories in the Old Testament and in the Hindu epic the Ramayana were probably several hundred years old before they were finally written down. The description of a religious story as myth can be controversial. Some followers of the faith regard as literally true a story that others regard as myth. So, for example, Christian fundamentalists believe that the world was created in six days, whereas other Christians see the story not as an historical account but as a myth containing the truth that God is the creator. Some theologians also describe historical incidents as mythologised; the supernatural and the natural have interacted, eternal time has been present in everyday history. Thus the life of Jesus is described as being mythologised because it has been given supernatural significance by Christians.

(b) Stories about the founders of the faith and key people of the faith
All faiths have within them stories about the key people of the faith. Why such stories are told within the faith varies according to the person featured. For example, Muslims believe that Muhammad though in every way human, lived out the teachings he had received from God in his everyday life. Thus Islamic lawmakers look to stories of Muhammad's life to determine how teachings in the Qur'an should be interpreted. On the other hand, while Moses and David are both heroes of the Jewish and Christian faith, neither Jew nor Christian would suggest that one should follow their lives in all things (Moses killed a man and David was an adulterer). Indeed one of the interesting things about both faiths is that they accept that fallibility is no bar to being a person of faith used by God. The status of Jesus in Christianity is also different from that of Muhammad in Islam. While Jesus is believed to be God incarnate, embodying all that is good and holy, only a very few Christians attempt to derive legal principles from his life. According to most scholars the gospel stories are told to portray Jesus as a man not only full of love, but also having the messianic power to heal the sick. They are essentially told to proclaim him as God's anointed one the 'Messiah'.

Nor are stories of people of the faith confined to the formative scriptural period but heroes and heroines continue to be made. Christianity, for example, has many stories about saints, Islam has its heroes and holy people.

The historicity of many of these stories about key religious people is another controversial issue. There is a double problem. First, the stories were often written down many years after the event, though this is not as big a problem as it might seem to the twentyfirst-century person used to having writing tools at their disposal. There was a strong emphasis on memory in the ancient world, with the accuracy of the oral tradition being carefully guarded, especially when it was about a major person and particularly with regard to things they actually said. Nevertheless, it is hard to maintain accuracy over time. Secondly, there is the problem that certain types of people attract certain types of stories. Thus key figures of faiths often have miraculous tales associated with their birth (e.g. there's usually a lot of light) and childhood (e.g. they display wisdom and learning at a young age). Thirdly, the traditions are selective – the community remembers what it wants to about the person in the light of their beliefs about him or her.

Whether or not stories from faith are accurate historically, they portray what the people in the faith believe about the person, how his or her significance has been understood. Moreover, there may be general historical truth in the way the character of the person is portrayed even though the detail may be of dubious historical value. Of course there are those in all faiths who believe in the literal truth of such stories.

(c) Legends

These bridge (b) and (d) and the line between myth and legend is a blurred one. Legends are told about substantiated historical figures and events or they accrue as folk tales. Some may be central to the faith, some more tangential. The legends about King Arthur, for example, portray him as a Christian king full of Christian virtue, but he is hardly a key religious figure. The main distinction between myth and legend is that the events of legend take place in time and are often about figures who were real people. Legends, also, often portray grand mythic qualities, such as the hero who fails through some tragic fault.

(d) Folk tales

These frequently begin 'Once upon a time...' or 'Once there was...' and unlike (a), (b) and (c), there is no attempt to root them in a certain time or place. Like myths and legends, they have an oral tradition behind them though writers have sometimes adopted their form. (e.g. the fairy tales of Oscar Wilde, Margaret Mahy, et al.). While folk tales are not generally found in scriptural canon, they may have an important function in passing on the belief and values of the community and with it the beliefs and values of the faith that has informed that community. Traditional Western fairy tales, for example, often have as central themes redemption, and the final triumph of good over evil, springing directly out of Christianity. This finality is frequently lacking in other traditions, which sometimes have a greater sense of the tragic or of the temporal nature of the victory. They may sometimes be set in an explicitly religious context, e.g. Sleeping Beauty with its Christening and godmothers, and Jewish folk tales which frequently contain references to the Sabbath, synagogues, rabbis and such like.

There are also classes of folk tales associated with types of people. Most if not all traditions have stories of the fool, e.g. the Muslim tale of the man who lost his keys in the gutter but searched for them on the doorstep because the light was better. The wise man and the trickster are other popular figures of tales found in many traditions. Their function is to remind the listener of wise and foolish ways to behave, and they too embody the values of the community that gave birth to them and kept them alive. Folk tales and some legends often cross cultural boundaries. This may be because the story has travelled, adapting itself to the new context. One example of the former is the story of the Russian Saint Josaphat, whose tale was instrumental in the conversion of the writer Leo Tolstoy. Josaphat was a Russian prince who was so moved by his encounter with a monk that he left his riches to lead the life of an ascetic in the desert. The history of the story can be traced through various versions to the story of the Indian prince Siddhartha Guatama, who left his riches and became the Buddha. Alternatively common human experiences may give rise to common themes, for example the story of the fool referred to above appears in several traditions.

(e) Didactic tales

While many stories have an implicit didactic function, some stories owe their existence to the requirements of teaching. The clearest example of this is parables, which are a popular teaching strategy of Judaism and one that Jesus, who was a Jew, used. Remember though, that parables are not morality tales. They do not demonstrate the consequences of an action. Rather they illustrate an idea. For example, if the story of the Prodigal Son were a morality tale, the moral would be 'Take your inheritance early, have a good time, and when you've spent it all and are down on your luck your old father will forgive you'. Rather, the Prodigal Son is told to illustrate the love of God for the outcast. A second example is allegories, when the characters and plot represent something else. (George Orwell's *Animal Farm* is a modern allegory). Thirdly, there are morality tales. The Victorians were fond of these, though the older Aesop's Fables are the better known example. Morality tales always carry the clear message 'If you behave like this, this is what will happen to you', e.g. the message of the Hare and the Tortoise is that slow and steady will win the race. The Victorian writer Hilaire Belloc parodied morality tales in his poems about the dreadful fates which befell children who were naughty.

Conclusion

Stories and poems are at the heart of human experience and are one of the first ways that people communicated with each other. They help people understand the world they live in and the relationships they have. Because of this, they are not only a form that young children can engage with, but are central to religious life and practice. Stories are a major vehicle for religions to communicate their understandings, beliefs and insights. We hope this guidance will provide you with a starting point for exploring religious literature, and, with it, religious questions, with children.

A SUMMARY OF **KEY POINTS**

> **Language and literacy are integral to religious understanding.**
> **Religious stories are an important and valuable way of presenting the world's religions to children.**
> **Religious stories offer children the opportunity to reflect on their own and others' experiences and find meaning in life.**
> **The key to the effective use of religious stories is preparation.**
> **Ensure you are familiar with the story and how you will handle it.**
> **Offer lots of opportunities for children to make their own responses.**
> **Children's literature can help you explore religious concepts and human experience themes with children.**

MOVING *ON* > > > > > > MOVING *ON* > > > > > > MOVING *ON*

Plan a lesson or sequence of lessons based on a religious story for your class or a class you taught on placement, using the principles outlined in this chapter.

5
Developing thinking skills in religious education

Chapter objectives

By the end of this chapter you will have developed knowledge and understanding of:

- **the importance of thinking skills in RE;**
- **central views regarding the development of children's thinking about religious and moral questions;**
- **ways of encouraging children to think critically in the context of RE;**
- **the potential for developing communities of enquiry in the context of RE.**

This chapter addresses the following Standards for QTS: **Q18 Q25a,b,c, Q30**

Introduction

Teaching children to think is essentially teaching them to be independent learners. We need to teach children enquiry skills, the capacity to reason and to make thoughtful judgements or we risk them leaving school limited to the knowledge acquired there, at the mercy of anyone who can tug at their emotions and limited by their own instant judgements. Teaching children to think is seen as part and parcel of the curriculum which should: *promote an enquiring mind and a capacity to think rationally... the curriculum should enable pupils to think creatively and critically, to solve problems...* (Curriculum, 2000)

In this chapter we see that teaching children RE is much more than filling their heads with information. It must also be about teaching them to be critical thinkers. One aim for RE is that children: *develop the ability to make reasoned judgements about religious and moral issues with reference to principal religions represented in Great Britain* (SCAA, 1994).

What is critical thinking?

The word 'critical' can seem a bit alarming and is not to be confused with being negative. Rather, the term 'critical thinking' is used instead as a contrast to lazy or sloppy thinking where someone says the first thing that comes into their head. By critical thinking skills we mean the forms of thinking that require the manipulation of concepts and information and not simply the recall of them. Much of the debate about what constitutes critical thinking has been informed by Bloom's Taxonomy (1956), an hierarchical classification system which places recall at the bottom of a pyramid and evaluation at the top.

Evaluation
Synthesis
Analysis
Application
Comprehension knowledge

These skills are sometimes presented as the segments of a wheel so as to move away from a hierarchy, albeit that most would put recalling knowledge as the most basic of skills.

PRACTICAL TASK PRACTICAL TASK **PRACTICAL TASK** PRACTICAL TASK **PRACTICAL TASK**

Type Bloom's Taxonomy into Google and search via Images. Compare ways people have expanded and elaborated the basic six skills.

Critical thinking and RE

It may surprise you that learning to think and reason is fundamental to RE; after all, reason and faith are often placed in opposite corners and brought out as sparring partners when writers such as Richard Dawkins, author of *The God Delusion* (2006,) and some brave bishop come into combat. It is true that some believers in all faiths have utter, unquestioning conviction which depends on submission to something they recognise goes against reason. And most believers would agree with T.S. Eliot (1955) that there are times when reasoning and questioning are set aside:

> You are not here to verify,
> Instruct yourself, or inform curiosity
> Or carry report. You are here to kneel
> Where prayer has been valid.

> (*Little Gidding*)

However, RE is neither worship nor induction into a belief system but a place where children can:

- grow in knowledge and understanding of faith and religion as they study different religious beliefs and practices (AT1);
- explore questions of identity, faith and morality in the light of their encounters with beliefs and practices, and their own experience (AT2).

Thinking skills are required in both these inter-related aspects of RE. The need to develop knowledge and understanding of religion and religious belief and practice continues throughout life. Encounter with religious phenomena does not stop at the school gate and nor is it confined to people who have an explicit religious commitment. The children you teach today will no doubt meet people of different religious convictions in their neighbourhoods and workplaces when they are grown up and they will come across religious items in the media. Newspapers will contain then, as they do now, articles about religion. Politics will still be affected by religious factions. Tomorrow's adults will need thinking skills to make sense of what they meet.

Thinking is also key to the process of reflecting on and exploring questions of meaning and purpose that arise out of the experience of being human. What is life about? Who am I? What happens when you die? What is good? These questions also occur in philosophy and this is often where the skills of philosophical education and RE overlap. The difference between them is that RE involves the religious/spiritual dimension and may draw on explicit religious teachings, practice and stories as a resource.

What part does reasoning play in answering these questions and what do we mean by reasoning? Reasoning and thinking are sometimes used interchangeably. In this chapter we are using reasoning as the process by which we come to make judgements – the reason is the justification we give for a viewpoint. A justification may be poor by being illogical and/or ill-informed or at the other end of the continuum it may be very logical, well-argued and well-informed. What constitutes a well-argued, logical well-informed decision may be disputed within different domains of enquiry, e.g. history, science, art. Each area has its own debates about appropriate methods of reasoning within the discipline. Within the realm of a particular religion, great emphasis is often placed on coherence and consistency within a given set of foundational beliefs. When RE takes place in a secular context we want children to develop reasoning based on their growing and changing understanding of the world and a foundational ethic of valuing and respecting themselves, others and the world around them. However, we also recognise that the sort of justifications they offer will reflect not only their limited experience of the world but the stage of their mental and physical development.

REFLECTIVE TASK

Reflect on yourself as a thinker. Do you accept everything that is said to you or do you try to fit it with other knowledge and experience? Are your views and opinions genuinely your own or do you simply regurgitate what you have heard? Remember you need to be a critical thinker yourself if you are going to teach critical thinking skills effectively.

Children's thinking skills

Before we can assist children in their development of thinking skills it is important to have some awareness of understanding of children as thinkers, especially in the fields of religion and morality. It was the Christian Apostle Paul who said: *When I was a child, I spoke like a child, I thought like a child, I reasoned like a child; when I became a man, I gave up childish ways* (1 Corinthians 13: 11). However, it was not until the twentieth century that child development became the focus of scientific enquiry. Sigmund Freud, the father of psycho-analysis, posited views on how adults had developed their concepts of God and codes of morality, seeing them rooted in the early dynamic of the family. Since then key names have dominated the debate about children's development with regard to religious and moral thinking and concepts.

- **Jean Piaget** (1968): systematic observations of his own children led Piaget to conclude that children moved through stages of reasoning that changed in kind as well as content, a movement that took place as a consequence of the development of the child's brain and the child's interaction with the world.
- **Lev Vygotsky** (Daniels, 2005): Vygotsky's work recognised the importance of language in learning how to think, giving a significant role to the adult or maturer child who by responding to the child at a level slightly higher than his current thinking (zone of proximal development) could scaffold his learning.
- **Margaret Donaldson** (1978): Donaldson indicated that children could use more sophisticated thinking if the tasks were embedded in contexts that were real and meaningful to them.
- **Lawrence Kohlberg** (1987): Kohlberg's research into children's moral reasoning led him to conclude that children move through three stages, each sub-divided into two to reach full maturity in their thinking about morality. According to Kohlberg people may get stuck at a stage in moral reasoning.
- **Carol Gilligan** (1982): a student of Kohlberg who critiqued Kohlberg from a feminist perspective and argued for the development of a morality of care, based on the sense of self.

- **Ronald Goldman** (1964): Goldman's highly influential research was on the religious reasoning of children, notably about children's concepts of God and beliefs about the Bible.
- **James Fowler** (1981): focused on children's faith development. His stage development theory is built on an understanding of faith as a search for meaning and purpose which is not confined to the explicitly religious sphere.
- **Robert Coles** (1990): Coles takes a psychoanalytical perspective on how children talk about spiritual matters.
- **Sylvia Anthony** (1940) and **Marie Nagy** (1959): examined children's understanding of death. Their work is the foundation for most work in this area.

It is not possible here to discuss the detail of each writer, or the research which has built on their work, some challenging conclusions, others offering different nuances. What follows therefore is what could be considered a general consensus about child development in these fields. This will enable you to meet Q18: *Understand how children and young people develop and that the progress and well-being of learners are affected by a range of developmental, social, religious, ethnic, cultural and linguistic influences.*

Children's thinking: Foundation and Key Stage 1

Young children have a wonderful capacity to respond to the world with awe and wonder. They will spontaneously gasp at a glimpse of the new moon in the sky, be intrigued by spider webs and take the time to stand and stare at a squirrel chomping away on nuts. They usually respond to stories imaginatively and fancifully, trusting what they are told is true without a division between the real and the made-up world – they don't worry about inconsistencies and create their own explanations for what is mysterious. Few question the possibility of Santa being everywhere at once – and delight in belief in him unless disillusioned by an older sibling.

Most Foundation and Key Stage 1 children will pay attention to one feature of a problem at a time ignoring the rest; they tend to have difficulty reversing things in their heads or holding more than one idea at the same time. They will often express what they want to be the case, rather than what is the case – one child in the class has a new puppy and suddenly so does everyone else. They will hotly deny that they have done something naughty but find it hard to lie on someone else's behalf. In their keenness to please they often say what they think the adult wants to hear.

Young children can be very sympathetic when someone is sad because they can respond to another's emotional state, and they know what may annoy a particular person but they usually find it hard to see something from another person's perspective unless the situation is very meaningful. Their moral reasoning is generally based on wrong being what is punished and right being what is rewarded or what pleases the adult. They are developing a sense of what is fair, albeit that their concern is about what is fair for them.

By the end of Key Stage 1 children are also possibly beginning to see that intention is a factor in morality. When they were younger they probably paid attention to volume and size rather than intention. For them, a child who dropped a large amount of cups was naughtier than one breaking a single cup when climbing to get a forbidden biscuit. However, when children reach six/seven they usually recognise intention as a factor.

They find it hard to handle ideas in abstract form. Ronald Goldman even went so far as to argue that children could not have any understanding of God because God is an abstract concept. Repeated studies seem to show that children have anthropomorphic ideas about God, seeing him as a Father Christmas figure in the sky. However, a consistent criticism of such research on children's concepts of God is that the questions asked or the task given invite an anthropomorphic response so it is difficult to judge the degree to which children think of God as a superhuman figure in the sky.

John Hull, in his small book *God-talk with Young Children* (1991), argues that young children have a concrete theology – they express their abstract ideas about God with concrete imagery, a precursor to metaphorical language about God: God is judge, father, light. Their flexible minds enable them to play with ideas and express new ones: *I don't think God was Jesus' father. I think he was Jesus' grandfather. He loved him but didn't live with him* (girl aged five and a half).

Ana-Maria Rizzuto (1979) suggests that most children have formed a god-representation by the time they are five in that they have concluded that there is a creator being usually called God. Everything must have been created – someone must have made the natural world since it wasn't made by humans, therefore God must have made it. Some children go on to ask the question that the philosopher Immanuel Kant believed undermined this cosmological argument for the existence of God: 'Who made God?' Many young children have a strong intimate sense of God as a companion, an invisible friend, with whom they can chat in play.

Few young children grasp the irreversible nature of death. One minute they seem to comprehend that the cat has died, the next minute they are out looking for it. They learn to live with the prolonged absence of a beloved family member feeling the repeated pain of hopes of a return dashed, rather than grief in the knowledge that they will never return.

Children's thinking: Key Stage 2

Around about the age of 6–7 children appear to make significant shifts in the manner of their thinking. They become aware of a division between fact and fiction, 'Did it really happen?', though the reason they question may surprise the adult. *I am not sure about Noah. The elephants would be too heavy for the plank.* They often look to the way a story is introduced to judge fact from fiction. A long time ago in a named city suggests fact but children are also beginning to question the more fantastical elements in a story. However, if the story is from their own religious tradition they are more likely to accept miracles without question. Angels inhabit their world sufficiently so as not to raise questions in the nativity story.

Their understanding of monotheism is often of tribal rather than universal monotheism: 'We have one God,' 'They have many gods.' Hindu children with their exposure to many images of God seem to be less locked into an image of God as the old man in the sky than children from a Christian background.

Key Stage 2 children are beginning to take others into account in their moral thinking. They often want to please others. They imbue rules of a game with a heavy authority. Whereas younger children will change rules arbitrarily, key stage children see rules in games as inviolable. They are starting to think about the intention of the miscreant rather than simply the effect of the action. Acceptable behaviour is often determined by what is acceptable amongst their peers, but there is also the appeal to the authority of the teacher, parent, law of the land, or the religious text. Stealing is wrong simply because it is against the law rather than because of reasoning based on hurt or offence.

At about age six children usually begin to understand that death is irreversible. They often then start to worry about what would happen to them if their parents died. At the same time many have a great curiosity about the body after death. Death is sometimes imaged as a person. Magical thinking about death may continue with children feeling responsible for a death, because of their thoughts and actions.

Religious and cultural backgrounds are also significant in the way children think and talk about religious matters. It is hardly surprising that a three-year-old informs his grandfather that he has just been talking to God about what happened at school, when that self-same grandfather is a devout Christian who prays with his grandchildren. David Heller's delightful study *The Children's God* (1986) explored how children's understanding of the character of God may be deeply influenced not only by the changing concerns of childhood but by the type of god-talk at home for example. The Jewish children in his study were more preoccupied with god as an actor in history than Christian Roman Catholic children for whom the family and forgiveness were stronger themes. But perhaps the biggest difference is between those from homes where god-talk is part of daily life and those who are not. The former seem to have much richer resources and a greater capacity to play with, and test out the idea of God and the themes of faith than the latter.

It may mean that the sense that they make of the religious world around them is puzzling to an adult as in this conversation by a group of 6–7-year-olds:

Child A: *Is Muhammad dead?*
Child B: *Yes, he lived a long time ago – everybody dies.*
[Other children nod in agreement]
Child C: *Everybody dies except Jesus. He's alive.*
Teacher: *Hmmm*
Child B: *Jesus dies every year at Easter but he comes alive at Christmas.*
Teacher: *Are you sure? What do the rest of you think?*
Others: *Yes Jesus comes alive at Christmas*
Teacher: *Jesus died on Good Friday and Christians think he came alive again on Easter Sunday.*
Children: *No, no, he dies every year at Easter and comes alive at Christmas.*

This is a common misconception, born perhaps of children's experience of the ritual of the Christian year. It was not one that the teacher could talk them out of, because it was a construction of their experience which made sense to them. Later in the school career they will no doubt have returned to the connection between Christmas and Easter.

But also consider the different levels of thinking in the following case study.

CASE STUDY

A group of seven-year-olds of Muslim and Christian backgrounds were discussing the Ancient Greek legend of Bacchus and Philemon. One asked whether the Greeks had a god. The teacher replied that they worshipped many gods. J. then said, ' We've got one God but some people have many gods.' Two Muslim children agreed, a third said firmly and repeatedly, 'No, there is only one God.'

Commentary: Here we see children reasoning in different ways. The final child may seem the most intolerant. However, given the general acuity of this child it seems more likely that she had recognised that belief in one God in Islam excludes the possibility of other gods whereas the other children thought in more limited tribal ways about God. Her abstract thinking has developed beyond that of her peers. One might hope that she would grow up valuing and respecting that people have different understandings of that one God. The point is that she was thinking through the issue.

PRACTICAL TASK PRACTICAL TASK PRACTICAL TASK PRACTICAL TASK PRACTICAL TASK

Find a picture that depicts a religious activity, e.g. children praying. Ask children what they think the children in the picture are doing and why they are doing it. Listen carefully and make notes about what concepts the children have and their manner of reasoning.

Implications of child development theories for teaching children to think in RE

The recognition that children develop in the way they reason has implications for your general teaching of RE but particularly the development of their thinking skills. These implications include the following.

- Objects, stories, pictures, puppets and DVDs are invaluable in encouraging thinking, instead of having children rely on memory of events or oral accounts. Tasks should be structured into small steps.
- Thinking activities need to be related to the child's experience, especially when working with younger children. It may be that the experience is an emotional one rather than a literal one. (See Chapter 4 on Stories.)
- The younger the child the more RE is focused on the practice-rituals, festivals, etc. and of a family belonging to a religion rather than the teachings of a religion. Talk of God will come out of stories and what the child of the faith practises.
- Children need lots of opportunities to speak about their ideas in a safe and secure environment.
- The teacher is a facilitator encouraging their thinking rather than having a determined outcome. Learning objectives will relate to the skills practised rather than specific knowledge gained. You will gently challenge their reasoning and justifications at a level they can comprehend rather than offering them reasons far beyond their comprehension.
- As a teacher who increasingly knows your child you will respond to the child as much as to the content of their answers. You might prod one child to extend their thinking including justifications whereas with another you may simply accept the thought.
- Remember that children are good at making up their own analogies but often find it hard to follow the analogies of an adult.
- Behaviour management strategies that involve discussion and reflection on the consequence of actions for others are to be preferred above reward and punishment systems. These can help prevent children getting stuck at a low level of moral reasoning.

Planning for thinking skills in RE

Some lessons will initially involve immersion in an experience of a story or visit; there needs to be the opportunity for the imagination and above all, awe and wonder, but as a general rule all lessons or units of lessons should involve the opportunity to think. When thinking about a lesson ask yourself when the children are going to have a chance to think and what sort of thinking will they be doing?

You can also use examples from the world of religion when you have to plan discrete lessons on thinking (see logic problems below).

Planning for thinking skills in RE 1: lessons with explicit planned reference to religious belief and practice

An investigative approach to the study of religion

A structured investigation building on curiosity enables children to develop the enquiry skills and the disposition to investigate for themselves. The basic structure of the sequence of lessons is as follows.

- Use something of interest or a stimulus to get the investigation started.
- Create the opportunity for asking questions, using what, when, who, why, how questions.
- Record the questions.
- Discuss where answers might be found (including whether any child knows an answer) and which answers would be difficult to find, e.g. it is not possible to find who made most artefacts but it is possible to find who uses them. Sources of information can be the internet, a visitor from the religion, a teacher or children in the school of that religion, a visit to a place of worship, a video or a DVD.
- Children investigate those sources.
- Discuss the reliability of the source.
- Record answers.
- Discuss how the various answers fit together.
- Identify further questions arising from the answers.

When identifying questions children are learning to **analyse**. When discussing the reliability of sources, children are learning to **evaluate**. When considering how answers fit together, children are learning to **synthesise**. When using their information for a project, they are learning to **apply** knowledge.

The following are some suggestions for starting points for investigations.

- Produce an artefact or artefacts, perhaps from a feely box and use it to generate questions. It is sensible to match your artefact to sources that you have available, i.e. non-fiction books, DVDs.
- Set up a database for an aspect of religion such as sacred books, or holy people. Identify key headings, e.g. When was it written? Who wrote it? What language?
- Set the class a challenge to find out about key dates for religion on a timeline. Help children move away beyond what happened, to where and how did people live and react to events, etc.
- Visit a place of worship and let the children draw what interests them rather than imposing a schedule on them (see Chapter 2 Encountering religion).
- Watch a video about the life of a child. The children think of three questions independently. They share questions with their group or partner and discuss whether the answers were in the video itself.

Use a class noticeboard to write questions and record answers as they are found. This doesn't have to be completed in one lesson but can be an on-going project.

It is also a good idea for an end product to be the stimulus for the research. These end products may be cross-curricular so that the skills of literacy or design technology are married to those of RE.

- Using a picture as a stimulus ask children to prepare for writing a diary about a child in the picture. What will they need to find out about the child's religion?
- Plan a menu which caters for the dietary requirements of travellers from different faiths. This could be for an airline or a restaurant or a birthday party. Children will need to investigate the food laws for the relevant faiths.
- Make dolls' houses in cardboard boxes belonging to people from different religious backgrounds. Children will need to generate questions about what is needed in them.
- The children make cards to send at a festival. They need to research the themes and stories associated with the festival.
- Build a drama around going on a pilgrimage. Children will need to research in order to prepare for their trip. You can build issues into the drama with tensions about whether the younger child should go on the trip or debates about the most ecological way to travel.

When children are younger and/or have limited reading skills you may need to do a class/or shared investigations. For example, if you have a restaurant in the structured play area you could read simple non-fiction books with the class to find out what a child of the faith could eat. Or if you are setting up the corner as the home for a Muslim family during Ramadan you could model researching the background information with the children. This can include looking at the names of the authors of the books and asking children how they think they found their information.

Comprehending (inference skills)

Inference is the art of reading between the lines – making considered guesses on the basis of the evidence available, whether it be text, picture or artefact. Broken glass on the floor and a cat locked in room and we can infer that the cat knocked the glass off the table. The pleasure of reading detective novels can be in the process of inference as the reader attempts to guess the murderer and the motive from the clues left by the author. Learning to infer from texts is an essential part of development of comprehension skills.

Inference about religious matters can be confusing since many religious practices are outside the ordinary and the everyday and may appear to contradict common sense behaviour. Indeed, archaeologists when faced with an object that completely puzzles them have been known to have recourse to the idea that it must be an object for use in ritual.

Nevertheless, we can use stories and pictures to help children develop inference skills. They can infer the feelings and motives of people in a story or a picture. They can suggest a prequel or sequel to the story, or what happened just before the picture was taken or what happened next. While these are primarily acts of imagination, the giving of reasons for their suggestions with reference to the story and the picture encourages more rigorous thinking skills (see also Chapter 4).

Artefacts and religious paintings are less easy to use to develop inference skills because a long history of symbolism often lies behind them and this is not always accessible to children. Even so, with careful questioning and an induction into some of the symbolism, they can infer information.

Look at a picture of the baptism of a baby. Ask children to suggest thought captions for the participants.

Look at Muslim children in a mosque school. Ask children what they think is happening and why.

Applying

Children are applying information when they use it to inform a new context or creation (see investigative skills above). They are also applying insights when they reflect or make links to their own lives. For example, they can reflect on feeling sorry and making amends after hearing the New Testament story of Zaccheus, who gave up being a tax collector after meeting Jesus. The end products described above after an investigation all involve the application of knowledge. So does playing in a role-play area set up as a home of a child from a particular religion.

Comparing and contrasting (analysing)

The importance of comparing and contrasting is discussed in Chapter 2 on encountering religion.

- Look at some examples of the same artefacts, preferably real objects but if this isn't possible, pictures – how are they similar but different? These objects could be, for example, Muslim prayer beads or Jewish mezuzahs or statues of the Hindu God Ganesh. Contrasts may be in the size, the material they are made of, or in the case of Ganesh, the posture. Finding what they have in common can point to what is essential in the object. At Easter you might use a joyful South American painting of a cross, adorned with symbols of life and joy and compare it with a crucifix showing a dying Jesus. What might each artist be trying to convey?
- A variation of the above is to compare objects with a similar purpose but with differences between religions. Prayer beads, for example, are used in Buddhism, Christianity and Islam. They vary in the number of beads, and the Christian beads usually also have a small crucifix, but they are all used for quiet prayer and meditation.
- Another variation can be made by having three objects and asking children to decide which two are similar and which one is different. The children are likely to come up with a number of ideas. They need to give their reasoning. An example might be a Jewish prayer shawl, Sabbath candles and an Advent candle ring. In this instance children will need to have met the objects before if the exercise is to say anything more than selecting out the piece of cloth.
- Compare and contrast the different feelings of characters in a scene in a story (see also Chapter 4).
- Look for similarities and differences in the retelling of a traditional story from a faith. Similarly compare and contrast illustrations of the story. This can lead to a discussion about why there are these differences. The Christian Christmas story particularly lends itself to this activity. This can be done with Key Stage 1 children (see below) and with much older children where contrasts in the age of the language can be drawn out.

CASE STUDY

Year 1 children were familiar with Dick Bruna's very simply and elegantly told *The Christmas Story* (1976). Mrs Jones then read them *Jesus' Christmas Party* (Allan 1993), which is told from the perspective of the innkeeper. She let them enjoy the story but then asked them how the two stories were similar. One child noticed that all the people in the stories looked quite poor.

- Older children can compare a written scriptural account taken from an accessible translation such as the *Good News Bible* with an image. They can discover for themselves that most stories of the Christian nativity are a conflation of accounts in the gospels of Matthew and Luke.
- Compare and contrast two or more places of worship after visits or through using images. These might be within the one religion – thus showing the diversity within the faith. You may not have access to two Hindu temples in your area but you can download images of Hindu temples from the web. Contrasts can be between architectural styles (often related to location), between whether purpose-built or an adaptation of a previous building, or between denominations. A Baptist church with its emphasis on preaching the word and often a baptismal font is quite different from a Roman Catholic church. Similarities and differences can also be made between faiths. You will need to draw out from the children those differences which they think are essential to the faith, and those which are incidental. (See also visiting a place of worship in Chapter 3 and information in the Appendix.)

Synthesising

Synthesising is learning to make connections between different pieces of information. If a question is open-ended children can often make insightful connections. When telling a religious story ask the children whether it reminds them of any other story they know and why: *it reminds me a bit of Snow White* (9-year-old having heard the Hindu Rama and Sita story for the first time). Or you might ask the children if this reminds them of anything they do: *We have a big meal on the temple on a Sunday* (7-year-old Sikh child after hearing about a Jewish family celebrating Shabbat).

You can also ask children to play with analogies and to create their own (See Chapter 4 on literacy), either in words or drawings. For example, if anger were a person what would he/she look like?

Ask children to use clues to bring together disparate pieces of information to make connections. This is a useful tactic for revision of knowledge and also gives the opportunity for both the teacher and the children to be creative in their ideas. There are no right answers, just good ones. For example, what connection might there be between a man hammering a small box onto a door frame and someone hurrying to the shops for some candles?

Evaluating

Bloom's taxonomy of thinking skills (1956) places Evaluating at the pinnacle of the pyramid – the most challenging of all the thinking skills. In practice many are quick to make judgements on the grounds of taste; it can be the first step not the last. Perhaps Bloom's pyramid is a reminder that evaluating should be the last step; a step which comes after thorough examination and thought. It is a skill that involves the weighing of arguments and the testing of their validity. (In RE in the primary school we are not in the business of encouraging children to make judgements about the worth of one religion against the other as though they were shopping for religion as they would shop for the best mobile phone provider; such a judgement is too complex for a primary school child.) However, they can evaluate statements against their knowledge and understanding. And they can evaluate opinions and moral arguments albeit at their own level of development. For example, after learning about the Sikh festival of Baisakhi children can be asked to evaluate the validity of statements.

Sikhs like to fight.
Guru Gobind Singh believed that all people were equal.

Or

It is okay to steal sweets from a shop because the shop owner has lots of sweets.

Logic problems

The capacity to think logically is essential in the study of all areas of disciplines and can be begun at Key Stage 2. Simple logic problems can be incorporated into RE to convey basic understanding or conversely religious subject matter can be included in logic problems. When introducing logic problems to children it is probably better to start with examples from immediate experience before moving on to explicitly religious ones. For example:

The apostle Paul, the founder of organised Christianity, celebrated Jewish Passover when he was a child.
Which religion came first, Judaism or Christianity?

Muslims believe that the Qur'an was first revealed to Muhammad.
The Qur'an speaks about events several centuries earlier, in the life of Jesus.
Who lived first, Muhammad or Jesus?

Also, discussion of fallacies (false arguments) can revise religious knowledge and extend understanding and challenge stereotyping. Children may find these difficult but at least it starts them talking and thinking. For example, ask the children what the problem is with these arguments:

Sikhs wear Turbans.
Amar wears a turban.
Therefore Amar is a Sikh.
(Other people than Sikhs wear turbans.)

Michelle is a Christian.
Michelle is nasty about people.
Therefore Christians are nasty about people.
(Michelle's nastiness is nothing to do with her being Christian.)

All Jewish men wear kappas.
David does not wear a kappa.
Therefore David is not a Jew.
(The argument is sound but the first statement/premise is false.)

PRACTICAL TASK PRACTICAL TASK PRACTICAL TASK PRACTICAL TASK PRACTICAL TASK

Using your knowledge of religion and the information in the appendix construct some logic tasks and validity questions based on these models. This task will help you develop your own knowledge and understanding of the religions concerned. For different models of false arguments type 'Fallacies' into Google.

Planning for thinking skills in RE 2: exploring questions of meaning and purpose

The exploration of questions of meaning and purpose requires the use of both critical thinking skills and creative thinking. The skills of critical thinking should give children well tuned 'crap detectors' (Postman, 1985) which enable them to test the claims of charismatic teachers and succulent advertising as they explore implicitly and explicitly questions such as who am I, what is life for, why be good, what happens when you die and is there a God? Creative thinking is necessary for their thinking to mature, as they allow their minds to play with new possibilities rather than being stuck with what they have always thought.

There are no fixed, right answers for any of these questions – none can be verified or proved – at least not in our lifetime. In faith schools teachers may, however, feel obliged to lead or prod children to the answers offered by the faith community; even so, if this is to be education, children need the space to question.

There are some general principles for discussion, whether it is a deliberately set up community of enquiry, the discussion at the end of a story or an incidental discussion prompted by an incident in class.

- Attentive listening is essential. Listening validates the speaker and may give him or her the confidence to articulate their ideas further. A child sharing their feelings or thoughts with you may feel hurt and slighted if it is clear that you are spending more time on disciplining another child in the class rather than listening to him. Too many of these experiences and the child is left feeling that what he has to say is not worth listening to. You can show that you have listened carefully by rephrasing what the child has said. This also helps other children to absorb what has been said.
- A slight 'Hmm' can encourage the child to say more.
- Encourage other children to respond to what has been said and to respond to the speaker rather than to you by asking whether anybody wants to add anything further, or do they disagree or have a question for the first speaker. This is quite different to the sort of circle time when children speak as individuals, unchallenged about their feelings. Circle time has its own worth in a different arena. Disagreement challenges and extends thinking. Learning to disagree politely and accept disagreement dispassionately is part of the process.
- Class sizes are not conducive to whole-class discussion, especially with young children. They are often dominated by a few confident individuals. These can often be very egoistical and want to speak about their own experience, rather than be responsive to others. It is hard for a whole class to pay attention and class management can become a problem. For this reason some of the best discussions take place in small groups round a table when the children may be engaged in another activity which stimulates spontaneous discussion. You can also plan for focused discussion with a small group while the rest of the class are doing self-directed activities.
- Be careful not to impose your views. It is easy for the know-all teacher to come in with her opinion which is likely to involve a level of argument beyond that of the child. It is here that Vygotsky's ideas on the zone of proximal development are so important. In the conversation the teacher can support thinking by asking a question that prods and scaffolds thinking. Other children's opinions are more likely to be within children's comprehension, especially when it comes to abstract ideas. Letting the conversation be controlled by the children, albeit facilitated by you, protects you from a child going home and telling her parents something about religious belief they object to.
- If your discussion is a formally set up one rather than spontaneous, remind the children of ground rules before you start. These ground rules can be established in a lesson at the beginning of the year when children discuss what makes a good discussion. At the end of a discussion, evaluate with the children

how well the discussion proceeded and whether the rules were obeyed. It is essential to create a safe place for discussion.

In thinking carefully about how you create opportunities for discussion and how you will listen and respond to children you are addressing Q25a,b. In creating a safe place for discussion you are addressing Q30.

Community of enquiry

The philosophy of the community of enquiry is based on the premise that real knowledge develops in communities with people listening to and challenging each other's ideas. It has been extensively developed by Robert Fisher (1990) and Matthew Lipman (1991), though the following has been adapted from work by Vivian Baumfield (2002).

The following procedure uses writing to encourage children to participate in discussion. You need to emphasise that this is writing for thinking and note-taking and they need to write quickly rather than concentrating on spelling and handwriting. Writing the statements on the board gives children thinking time and helps keep them focused. If you are working on an interactive whiteboard you will have a record afterwards.

1 Ask children to write down, by themselves, all the things they can think about to do with a key issue, for example jealousy, love, happiness, faith, forgiveness.
2 Children move into groups and share what they have written. Ask them then to write a joint opinion in the form of a statement about the subject.
3 Select one statement at random. Write it on the board.
4 Children respond as individuals by writing down whether they agree or disagree with the statement and why (this is most important).
5 Select one child and write down their response on the board.
6 Repeat this a couple more times until it feels as though you really have a discussion going.

The strategy of beginning with writing helps bring in a lot of children who might otherwise not engage with a discussion. It also emphasises the need to respond to what has just been said rather than making one's own point.

Most study of religions should have a theme/topic which emerges as the basis for reflection/discussion.

Other starting points for a community of enquiry

- Look at a character in a story. Ask children to formulate an opinion on his/her behaviour and choices and then discuss it.
- Take a key theme arising from a religious story and develop it further.
- Create a dramatic scenario in which children act in role to address problems or issues.
- Work together as a class to make up a daily or weekly soap opera. Having established a setting, children suggest problems and conflicts for the characters and discuss the way forward. Another form of this activity is to create chance cards to which the children have to respond with the next part of the story, e.g. Ryan sees his friend hitting his younger brother; Ella's mother wants her to have the baby christened but Ella thinks it is hypocritical.

- Take a saying from a scripture or a proverb and discuss with the class, moving from pairs to small groups, e.g. 'It is better to give than to receive' or 'Love those that hate you'. Children can write stories to illustrate the proverbs.
- Put children into a situation where they have to justify choices and opinions, e.g. class vote on the greatest hero of all time with children providing a case for 'their hero'.
- Analyse the positive and negative qualities of the same phenomenon. With younger children this can be something physical such as cats, or giving presents. Older children can discuss abstract ideas such as anger or compassion. This is a good activity to incorporate into learning about Hinduism as Hindu stories seldom divide into neat opposing camps. Even the ten-headed demon in the Rama and Sita story told at Diwali has some good qualities.

CASE STUDY

Year 6 were studying the five Ks of Sikhism, focusing on the theme of protection. The class teacher asked them to consider which groups in society needed protection. One group suggested 'old people'. Rather than simply accepting the suggestion the teacher asked for further comment. Who agreed or disagreed? This led to an interesting discussion about many old people wanting to be listened to rather than just looked after.

Conclusion

A good day at school is one which children have enjoyed but also one in which their thinking has been developed and challenged. The best days are when they go on talking and thinking about their ideas at home. We hope that this chapter has given you lots of ideas to get them thinking.

A SUMMARY OF **KEY POINTS**

> Learning to think is an important dimension of RE.

> Children develop in the way they think and in the way they respond to religious questions.

> The teacher's role is to listen and to encourage children to offer reasons and to think about them further.

> Teachers should not impose their reasoning on children.

> Thinking skills can be incorporated into RE and examples from religious beliefs and practices can be used in discrete thinking skills lessons.

> The community of enquiry can use a variety of starting points including drama.

MOVING *ON* > > > > > > MOVING *ON* > > > > > > MOVING *ON*

Plan carefully a discussion activity into your next unit of work using drama or story as your stimulus.

6
The contribution of RE to children's personal and spiritual development and well-being

Chapter objectives

By the end of this chapter you will have developed knowledge and understanding of:

- how the Every Child Matters agenda impacts on the teaching of RE;
- the role RE has to play in:
  - children's spiritual, moral, social and cultural development
  - children's personal, social and health education
  - global citizenship and social justice;
- planning and teaching aspects of personal development through RE.

This chapter addresses the following Standards for QTS: **Q1, Q2, Q10, Q14, Q15, Q18, Q19, Q25a**

Introduction

Although the National Curriculum addresses children's academic needs and develops their understanding of specific areas of the curriculum such as mathematics and English, it does not represent the whole of the work we do with children in school. The Every Child Matters agenda, requires us not only to contribute to children's ability to enjoy and achieve (see links to this in Standards Q10 and Q15), but also draws our attention to children's wider lives and experiences and their sense of well-being (see links to this in Standards Q1, Q2 and Q25a).

Over the years a range of terms have been used to describe this wider aspect of children's lives. These include: Spiritual, Moral, Social and Cultural Education (SMSC), Personal Social and Health Education (PSHE), Citizenship Education, Global Citizenship, Education for Sustainable Development, Education for Social Justice, Values Education, Emotional Development, among others. It is the responsibility of schools to ensure that these themes are addressed in all aspects of school life, from the school's mission statement and policies through to lesson planning. All subjects in the curriculum have a role to play in these areas, and it could be argued that RE has a pivotal role. In this chapter we will explore how RE can contribute to children's understanding and development in these wider aspects of their education.

It is important to note that there is a good deal of overlap between all these themes, and we should not concern ourselves too much about whether something is moral or social, cultural or spiritual. Rather we must recognise that all our interactions with children will help shape the people they are and the people they will become. We must therefore be aware of the messages and values we communicate with children each time we work with them.

Rather than trying to plan separate lessons for these themes and areas, it is better to identify them in the work that is already being planned for the children. If we begin from the assumption that everything we do with the children affects their personal development in some way or other, then we will not be saying *'does* this work contribute?' but *'in what ways* does it contribute?'

During the planning process therefore, opportunities to recognise *how* the work contributes to children's personal development should be considered. Most importantly, space should be given for the children to *respond* to the material they are studying, so that they can share their views and opinions about it. This is what the RE QCA Attainment Target 2 is all about (see Chapter 1).

Attending to children's personal development, then, focuses our attention not only on the content of RE but also the teaching strategies we use (see Chapters 2 and 3 for more information on pedagogy).

Below are descriptions of some of the ways in which RE can contribute to the personal development and well-being of children.

RE and SMSC

Under the terms of the 1988 Education Reform Act all schools must contribute to children's spiritual, moral, social and cultural education. The Standards also remind us that teachers must know how children's progress and well-being is affected by a range of influences and need to provide for these (see Q18 and Q19).

How are these terms to be understood? It could be said that 'moral education' refers to our responsibility to help children make decisions about how to treat themselves and others. 'Social education' helps children to understand the relationships between themselves and others, while 'cultural education' helps them to explore their own sense of belonging and how that might be similar or different to that of others.

Each of the terms is open to a variety of interpretations, and the term 'spiritual' is probably the most elusive of them. In a doctoral study by McCreery (2000) involving 162 teachers, over 90 different definitions were used to talk about it. It is important for each teacher to consider his or her own definition of it to understand how it will feature in RE work. In 1995, a SCAA discussion paper suggested that the spiritual:

> *needs to be seen as applying to something fundamental in the human condition which is not necessarily experienced through the physical senses and/or expressed through everyday language. It has to do with relationships with other people and, for believers, with God. It has to do with the universal search for individual identity -with our responses to challenging experiences, such as death, suffering, beauty, and encounters with good and evil. It is to do with the search for meaning and purpose in life and for values by which to live.*
>
> (SCAA, 1995, p6)

PRACTICAL TASK PRACTICAL TASK PRACTICAL TASK PRACTICAL TASK PRACTICAL TASK

Consider what you understand the term 'spiritual development' to mean.

● What is your understanding of 'spiritual'?

● What does being 'spiritually developed' mean?

● What role do you see yourself having in children's spiritual development?

There are different aspects of spirituality that can be explored in RE:

● investigating the spiritualities of specific religious traditions;
● studying the lives of people who are considered to be 'spiritually enlightened';
● discussing our own responses to spiritual matters;
● studying the ways in which people have expressed spiritual aspects (through the arts, for example).

CASE STUDY

Claire's Year 5 class had been studying how God is seen in Christianity and Sikhism. They had looked at some of the stories from each of the traditions which offered insight into the nature of God and they had chatted to visitors from the local church and gurdwara about what God meant to them. The children had commented about the similarities between the two faiths. The next task Claire gave them was for them to think of questions they would ask God if they were a Christian or a Sikh. Claire wanted to know if the children would draw on what they had learned to generate their questions.

Working in groups of four, the children talked about what questions they might ask. They listed all their questions on paper and were to decide between them which was the most important question. One group listed the following:

1 *Why do some people do horrible things?*
2 *Is there a devil?*
3 *What is heaven like?*
4 *Do animals go to heaven?*
5 *Why did you make the world?*
6 *What do you look like?*
7 *How can you see all the world at the same time?*

They chose question 5 as their most important one.

Claire gathered each group's question and displayed them for the whole class. She said they would have a discussion on one or two of the questions. The following day the children chose three questions to discuss. Claire gave them time to jot down their own thoughts about each question before they began the discussion.

Opportunities should also be found in RE for children to respond in *awe and wonder* to the material we are presenting them with. The learning context can be planned in a way that sets an appropriate atmosphere for engaging with the children's imagination. For example, the telling of a story can be a fairly straightforward event, but if planned carefully can transfix the children, so that the story-telling becomes more of an experience than just a classroom experience.

> **CASE STUDY**
>
> Rebecca was introducing the children in her Nursery to the Hindu Diwali story of Rama and Sita and their encounter with the demon Ravanna. As the children returned from afternoon play, they found the classroom in darkness, except for a row of tiny lights at the front of the room. From somewhere in the dim light, some gentle Indian music was playing. The children began to speak in excited whispers as they settled themselves on the carpet. At the front of the room was a screen made out of a white sheet and beside this Rebecca sat waiting for the children to settle.
>
> As they did, she began to tell a story, 'A long time ago in the land of India lived a prince and his beautiful wife . . .' As the story began a light came on behind the screen and two shadow puppets began to dance across their stage. As Rebecca told the story, the children listened in rapt attention. Hardly a sound could be heard as the story unfolded with only the tinkling music as accompaniment.

RE and PSHE

Closely related to SMSC is children's Personal, Social and Health Education (see Standards Q18 and Q19). This links closely to aspects of the Every Child Matters agenda which high-lights our responsibilities for children's health and well-being and their future lives.

RE plays a significant part in promoting PSHE through children:

- developing confidence and responsibility and making the most of their abilities;
- learning about what is fair and unfair, right and wrong, and being encouraged to share their opinions;
- developing a healthier, safer, lifestyle by learning about religious beliefs and teachings about drugs, food and drink, leisure, relationships and human sexuality;
- developing good relationships and respecting the differences between people by learning about the diversity of different ethnic and religious groups;
- learning about the destructive power of prejudice, challenging racism, discrimination, offending behaviour and bullying;
- being able to talk about relationships and feelings;
- considering issues of marriage and family life and meeting and encountering people whose beliefs, views and lifestyles are different from their own.

PRACTICAL TASK PRACTICAL TASK PRACTICAL TASK PRACTICAL TASK PRACTICAL TASK

Using a school's RE curriculum or Locally Agreed Syllabus for both Key Stages 1 and 2, identify where each of the aspects above are dealt with in RE.

RE and global citizenship

Global citizenship (GC) is a dimension to the primary curriculum which ensures children acquire an understanding of their place and significance as individuals and members of British society in the wider global context. This relates to the values underlying the curriculum, curriculum content and the teaching and learning methodologies.

The values underlying the curriculum need to be based in concepts of equal opportunities, rights and responsibilities and creating a caring and cohesive community. In relation to content each aspect of the curriculum can incorporate a global dimension, e.g. stories from world literature as well as English-language ones. The approach to teaching and learning includes participatory and child-centred learning. The content, values and methods represent an approach to learning that is based in the knowledge, understanding, skills and attitudes which will not only develop the individual but contribute to the well-being of the local and global community.

PRACTICAL TASK PRACTICAL TASK **PRACTICAL TASK** PRACTICAL TASK **PRACTICAL TASK**

To explore your own understanding of global citizenship find different ways of completing this sentence:

'A global citizen is one who...'

The National Framework for RE (QCA, 2004, p25) recognises that RE can promote citizenship by:

- developing children's knowledge and understanding about the diversity of national, regional, religious and ethnic identities in the UK and the need for mutual respect and understanding;
- enabling children to think about topical spiritual, moral, social and cultural issues including the importance of resolving conflict fairly;
- exploring the rights, responsibilities and duties of citizens locally, nationally and globally;
- enabling children to justify and defend orally and in writing personal opinions about issues, problems and events.

In March 2005 the DfES (in association with the DFID and several other bodies) published guidance for head teachers, governors, local education authorities and teachers in *Developing the Global Dimension in the School Curriculum* (DFID, DfES et al, 2005). In relation to RE it suggests that at Key Stage 1:

Children learn that people in their own community and around the world have diverse belief systems and recognise similarities between them. By doing this they can begin to develop an awareness and respect for different points of view.

(DFID, DfES et al., 2005, p11)

At Key Stage 2:

Children learn about the world's major religions and about how each individual is important. By doing this they can appreciate religious diversity in their own society and around the world. They can learn about others' diverse religious beliefs with regard to the environment and how religion impacts upon people's lives.

(DFID, DfES et al, 2005 p13)

This document identifies the 8 concepts of global dimension as, global citizenship, interdependence, conflict resolution, sustainable development, diversity, social justice, values and perceptions and human rights. Some aspects of these concepts can be delivered through RE as shown in the following chart.

The eight key concepts within the global dimension in the school curriculum and how they can be delivered through RE

Key concepts	Taught in RE
Global citizenship Gaining the knowledge, skills and understanding of concepts and institutions necessary to become informed, active, responsible citizens: • developing skills to evaluate information and different points of view on global issues through the media and other sources • learning about institutions, declarations and conventions and the role of groups, NGOs and governments in global issues • developing understanding of how and where key decisions are made • appreciating that young people's views and concerns matter and listened to; and how to take responsible action that can influence and affect global issues • appreciating the global context of local and national issues and decisions at a personal and societal level • understanding the roles of language, place, arts, religion in own and others' identity	Analysis of the media, e.g. BBC's *Newsround* programme, looking for values and perceptions underlying selection and presentation of news items Participating in community environmental projects Exploring their own identity through affirmation exercises and learning about family life in various religious communities in UK and wider world Finding out about the work of charitable organisations linked to religious traditions such as the Red Crescent and Christian Aid Looking at and responding to the arts in particular religions
Interdependence Understanding how people, places, economies and environments are all inextricably interrelated, and that choices and events have repercussions on a global scale: • understanding the impact of globalisation and that choices made have consequences at different levels, from personal to global • appreciating the links between the lives of others and children's and young people's own lives • understanding the influence that diverse cultures and ideas (political, social, religious, economic, legal, technological and scientific) have on each other and appreciating the complexity of interdependence • understanding how the world is a global community and what it means to be a citizen • understanding how actions, choices and decisions taken in the UK can impact positively or negatively on the quality of life of people in other countries	Moral decision-making activities Look at the contents of a shopping bag and labels on clothing to see how much these basic items link them to other parts of the world. Link this to the concept of 'tawhid' (the oneness of God) in Islam, or in the Buddhist and Hindu concepts of the oneness and interdependence of the universe Consider the similarities and differences between themselves and the children they study

Conflict resolution

Understanding the nature of conflicts, their impact on development and why there is a need for their resolution and the promotion of harmony:

- knowing about different examples of conflict locally, nationally and internationally and different ways to resolve them
- understanding that there are choices and consequences for others in conflict situations
- understanding the importance of dialogue, tolerance, respect and empathy
- developing skills of communication, advocacy, negotiation, compromise and collaboration
- recognising conflict can act as a potentially creative process
- understanding some of the forms racism takes and how to respond to them
- understanding conflicts can impact on people, places and environments locally and globally

Exploring classroom conflicts and the various ways in which they might be resolved in circle time

Listening to people from other faiths and expressing thoughts and feelings

Asking questions to clarify misunderstandings about faith traditions and learn from some of the stories in faith traditions about ways to resolve conflict and overcome hatred.

Developing empathy with children from other cultures with different ethnicity and learning how to appreciate diversity.

Sustainable development

Understanding the need to maintain and improve the quality of life now without damaging the planet for future generations:

- recognising that some of the earth's resources are finite and therefore must be used responsibly by each of us
- understanding the interconnections between the social, economic and environmental spheres
- considering probable and preferable futures and how to achieve the latter
- appreciating that economic development is only one aspect of quality of life
- understanding that exclusion and inequality hinder sustainable development for all
- respecting each other
- appreciating the importance of sustainable resource use – rethink, reduce, repair, re-use, recycle – and obtaining materials from sustainably managed sources

Developing a sense of awe and wonder at the natural world

Discovering the various teachings on looking after the animals and the environment in different religious traditions

Exploring the consequences of action in relation to the future of the planet

Listening to stories that challenge the acquisition of wealth as the source of happiness

Guided meditation on the beauty and wonder of the earth

Learning to treasure and value what you have

Listening to each other's experiences and opinions with respect

Diversity

Understanding and respecting differences and relating these to our common humanity:
- appreciating similarities and differences around the world in the context of universal human rights
- understanding the importance of respecting differences in culture, customs and traditions and how societies are organised and governed
- developing a sense of awe at the variety of peoples and environments around the world
- valuing biodiversity
- understanding the impact of the environment on cultures, economies and societies
- appreciating diverse perspectives on global issues and how identities affect opinions and perspectives
- understanding the nature of prejudice and discrimination and how they can be challenged and combated

Learning about the similarities and differences between world religions and the diversity within them

Studying case studies of families from different cultures living in the United Kingdom and how religion shapes their lives, their beliefs and way of life

Appreciation of the variety and achievements and ways of overcoming adversity

Moral education – exploring teachings on prejudice and the dangers raised by this

---

Social justice

Understanding the importance of social justice as an element in both sustainable development and the improved welfare of all people:
- valuing social justice and understanding the importance of it for ensuring equality, justice and fairness for all, within and between societies
- recognising the impact of unequal power and access to resources
- appreciating that actions have both intended and unintended consequences on people's lives and appreciating the importance of informed choices
- developing the motivation and commitment to take action that will contribute to a more just world
- challenging racism and other forms of discrimination, inequality and injustice
- understanding and valuing equal opportunities
- understanding how past injustices affect contemporary local and global politics

Studying the lives of individuals – some great religious leaders who, inspired by faith, sought to bring justice and equality to the world: Gandhi, Martin Luther King, Guru Gobind Singh, etc.

Examining religious discrimination in the past and the present

Considering rights and responsibilities within the religious traditions

Exploring concepts of power and authority

Human rights

Knowing about human rights, including the UN Convention on the Rights of the Child:

- valuing our common humanity, the meaning of universal human rights
- understanding rights and responsibilities in a global context and the interrelationship between the global and the local
- understanding that there are competing rights and responsibilities in different situations and knowing some ways in which human rights are being denied and claimed locally and globally
- understanding human rights as a framework for challenging inequalities and prejudice such as racism
- knowing about the UN Convention on the Rights of the Child, the European declaration on Human Rights and the Human Rights Act in UK law
- understanding the universality and indivisibility of human rights

Examining the laws and teachings of specific religious traditions and what they reveal about how humankind is viewed

Exploring how people's religious responsibilities can be integrated with life in the UK and the issues this might raise

Values and perceptions

Developing a critical evaluation of representations of global issues and an appreciation of the effect these have on people's attitudes and values:

- understanding that people have different values, attitudes and perceptions
- understanding the importance and value of human rights
- developing multiple perspectives and new ways of seeing events, issues, problems and opinions
- questioning and challenging assumptions and perceptions
- understanding the power of the media in influencing perceptions, choices and lifestyles
- understanding that the values people hold shape their actions
- using different issues, events and problems to explore children and young people's own values and perceptions as well as those of others

Examining religious teachings and texts to identify and discuss the values that underpin them

Having conversations with members of different faith traditions about what is important to them

Exploring how religious belief informs perceptions of the world and how to live within it

Identifying and developing their own beliefs and values

Exploring 'rights' and 'responsibilities' with children in RE

> ### CASE STUDY 1
>
> Peter asked his Year 5 class to work in groups and make a list under the heading 'Things we need to make us happy'. After some minutes he asked the groups to share their lists. Without making any comment, he then asked the groups to divide their list into two, under the headings of 'Wants' and 'Needs'. As Peter circulated around the groups he found that the children were discussing the lists carefully and were able to justify why things belonged in each category. One group's work looked like this:
>
> | Wants | Needs |
> |-------|-------|
> | Computer | Food |
> | To go to Spain | Drink |
> | Nice clothes | Clothes |
> | New trainers | A home to live in |
> | Television | A mum and dad |
>
> From this work Peter introduced the children to children's rights and asked them to draw up a charter that would apply to any child in the world. The class then compared their work to the United Nations Convention on the rights of the child to see how far it matched their own charters.
>
> Following on from this work, the class split into groups to find out about the work of different charitable organisations from religious traditions, to see how they help children around the world to receive what they need.

PRACTICAL TASK PRACTICAL TASK **PRACTICAL TASK** PRACTICAL TASK **PRACTICAL TASK**

Select one world religion and do some research to find out what teachings it has about humankind's relationship to the natural world. Use this to plan a series of lessons for a Key Stage 1 or Key Stage 2 class on the theme of 'Caring for our world'.

RE and social justice

As teachers we have a responsibility both to model the values associated with social justice and to help children develop an awareness of how it affects their lives. The Standards draw our attention to these, saying that teachers must:

> *have high expectations of children and young people including a commitment to ensuring that they can achieve their full educational potential and to establishing fair, respectful, trusting, supportive and constructive relationships with them (Q1);*
>
> *demonstrate the positive values, attitudes and behaviour they expect from children and young people (Q2);*
>
> *teach lessons and sequences of lessons across the age and ability range for which they are trained in which they use a range of teaching strategies and resources, including e-learning, taking practical account of diversity and promoting equality and inclusion (Q25a).*

From an early age, children develop a keen sense of what is 'fair' and 'unfair'. This can be our starting point for exploring social justice in RE. Any age group can begin by thinking about their own experiences of fairness. They can talk about what 'fair' and 'unfair' mean to them. The teacher might read them stories which demonstrate these two concepts for further discussion. The work can then be developed into explicitly religious contexts such as:

- reading stories from religion that demonstrate fairness and unfairness;
- examining the teachings of the world faiths about how we treat others;
- studying the ways in which religious groups have been persecuted in the past;
- studying which religious groups are persecuted or discriminated against today;
- examining the lives of religious teachers and figures who fought for social justice;
- exploring how people of different religious traditions fight for social justice today.

At each stage the children should be encouraged to identify their role in promoting social justice in the world today. How would they respond if someone discriminated against them? How would they respond if they witnessed someone abusing someone else?

CASE STUDY

Below is a lesson plan which was the third of a series of lessons for a Year 3 class around the theme 'Fairness and Friendship'.

Lesson title: The work of Mahatma Gandhi

Prior learning: The children have studied a unit on Hinduism and are familiar with some of the beliefs and values. They have explored the notion of 'Karma' and are aware of the notion of our actions affecting the world around us and ourselves.

Lesson objectives: By the end of the lesson the children will:
- be aware of Gandhi's concern for the poor in India
- be familiar with Gandhi's work for reform
- be able to express their own views about the world's poor.

Lesson content
1. Revise previous week's work on fairness – in pairs, complete the sentences:
   It's fair when...
   It's not fair when...
2. Remind children of previous work on Hinduism – what do they remember?
3. Tell the Hindu myth of the creation of people, explaining how this has influenced Hindu society. Ask for responses to the story and its impact. What do they think about it?
4. Introduce Gandhi as someone who was unhappy with how the poor were treated. Display images of Gandhi and briefly describe his work.
5. Use a quote from Gandhi to begin a discussion: *We must become the change we want to see.*

Discussion: Who are the poor in our society? What is done to help them? What can I do to help? Work in small groups to discuss.

Lesson conclusion
Gather thoughts of each group and display.
Take suggestions for ways in which our class could help the poor in our society both locally and globally.

Next lesson
Examine possibilities for charitable work in the local community/global community
Follow up suggestions made by the children.

Conclusion

In all the work we plan to do with children, we need to keep in mind why it is of value to them as people. How does the work help them to understand themselves and the world they live in? How does it help them to make sense of what they see, hear and experience? How does it help them develop a strong sense of identity which will help them to encounter the wider world? We need to be able to answer these questions in order to be sure that the work we plan for them is relevant to their present lives and will help them thrive and succeed as they grow.

A SUMMARY OF **KEY POINTS**

> The National Curriculum represents only part of the work we do with children in school.

> All the work we do with children should contribute to their personal development and well-being.

> RE has a significant role to play in children's personal development.

> The planning process in RE should include reference to how the work might contribute to children's personal development.

> RE enables children to become aware of the wider world and global issues.

> RE can contribute to the global dimension of the school curriculum.

MOVING *ON* > > > > > > MOVING *ON* > > > > > > MOVING *ON*

Look at the next unit of work you are planning in RE. Is there an opportunity for exploring issues of global citizenship or social, spiritual and moral development?

7
RE in the Early Years

Chapter objectives

By the end of this chapter you will:

- **appreciate the value of RE in young children's education;**
- **be able to identify children's starting points in RE and use them to assist planning;**
- **understand how RE fits into the wider Early Years curriculum;**
- **be able to integrate RE learning into Early Years planning.**

This chapter addresses the following standards for QTS: **Q5, Q10, Q14, Q15, Q18, Q19, Q22, Q25**

Introduction

This chapter explores the value of RE in young children's education and considers the content and approaches that best meet young learners' needs. We will explore how young children learn in RE and what you can do to contribute to children's development in this area. We will also consider the limitations of what we can do in RE and demonstrate how a good knowledge and understanding of children's development can help us to plan appropriate work for them. The chapter will demonstrate how the QTS Standards can be met in relation to the teaching of children in the Early Years Foundation Stage (EYFS).

The principles in teaching RE outlined in Chapter 2 apply to teaching in the Early Years Foundation Stage, although not in all the examples. Re-read Chapter 2 and the section on young children's thinking in Chapter 5 in preparation for teaching in the Foundation Stage.

Children in the Foundation Stage and religion and spirituality

Children in the Foundation Stage have experiences of rituals such as birthdays and festivals, albeit their memories of specific events may be dim. Some will have been inside places of worship if only for a wedding or funeral and some will come from homes where prayer is a part of daily life. The children are being inducted into their family's way whether explicitly religious or not and whether that family is just the child and a parent, or a whole extended family. They will also be imbibing the family values.

Unless it has been sadly already quashed, they will bring to school inquisitiveness about the world around them, and a desire to know 'why'. All those questions form part of the quest for meaning, some more obviously so with respect to religion than others. Those questions are variants of such questions as 'Why can't I do what I want?' (moral responsibility), 'Who made the tree?' (creation), 'Why does it hurt?' (suffering in the world).

Their love of fantasy and their need for play is a gift; you can enrich them with stories and create spaces for them to play with religion. You will want to nurture their capacity for awe and wonder.

But you will also need to remember that they are young children. Most find it very difficult to follow explanations about abstract matters. They do not have the experiences or the language to deal with explicitly religious concepts when the teacher is in the lead in the conversation though they may raise things themselves. Above all remember that they learn best through play.

RE and the Early Years Foundation Curriculum

The Standards require teachers to: *have a secure knowledge and understanding of their subjects/curriculum areas and related pedagogy to enable them to teach effectively across the age and ability range for which they are trained* (Q14). This means that as we approach RE in the Early Years we need to be confident in what we are to teach and how.

The first question to ask is: Why do we think RE is a valuable aspect of human experience for young children to begin to study? Surely it is far too complex and abstract for them to understand? RE for primary-aged children has been a legal requirement since 1944 (see Chapter 1), and while it is not a statutory requirement at the Early Years Foundation Stage Curriculum there are elements of it within the EYFS.

The EYFS curriculum is the one which QCA has identified as being suitable for children in the earliest years of schooling. As teachers we must: *know and understand the relevant statutory and non-statutory curricula, frameworks, including those provided through the National Strategies, for their subjects/curriculum areas, and other relevant initiatives applicable to the age and ability range for which they are trained* (Q15).

This curriculum addresses different aspects of children's development. Within this frame-work, RE does not have a specific place. However, several of the areas of learning offer valuable opportunities for RE and teachers can easily integrate RE themes within these areas and use RE to contribute to other areas of learning (see Chapter 8 on Planning). The chief areas that RE can contribute to are:

- Personal, social and emotional development;
- Knowledge and understanding of the world;
- Communication, language and literacy;
- Creative development.

However, there are also links with aspects of physical, problem-solving, reasoning and numeracy development, as can be seen in some of the examples below.

Personal, social and emotional development

RE contributes to this area of the curriculum in several aspects: self-confidence and self-esteem, disposition and attitudes, relationships, behaviour and self-control, and sense of community. Through RE the children will begin to reflect on their own lives and experiences, discuss their feelings, beliefs and cultural influences. They will also start to become aware of the perspective of others, both through sharing their experiences with their classmates and through being introduced to other beliefs and traditions by the teacher.

This in turn will develop children's confidence so that they are able to contribute to discussion, sharing ideas. Drawing on their own experiences, and that of others, will encourage engagement and concentration. The range of materials and approaches used in RE should therefore be interesting and varied, capturing the children's imagination.

A focus on others in RE encourages the children to see the world from others' perspectives and demonstrate to them the need for shared values and codes of behaviour. They will recognise that communities follow such guidelines, and may have distinctive teachings that influence behaviour and lifestyle.

CASE STUDY

Mrs Jones wanted the children to think of themselves and individuals with their own thoughts values and beliefs. She sat the children in a circle and asked them to finish the sentence: 'My name is... and I like to....' She acted as a model first: 'My name is Mrs Jones and I like to dig in the garden.' Keith said, 'My name is Keith and I like to eat chips.' Ella said, 'My name is Ella and I like to play cricket.' Hafsa said, 'My name is Hafsa and I like to look at books.'

Encouraging children to share their names in this manner contributes to their sense of identity, a key aspect of RE. As names often have religious and cultural links this type of activity can be used as a prelude to introducing children to different backgrounds than their own.

Knowledge and understanding of the world

RE contributes to this area through exploring a sense of time, a sense of place, cultures and beliefs. Links to the past in RE will include drawing on stories from the religious traditions, in particular those related to key figures or events. More personally, the children can examine their own past, their birth and growing up, and the past of people in their family and community. RE also encourages children to think about the world around them, the world of nature and places that might be special to them and others. They can begin to consider their own and other communities – what features are significant and where religion has an impact on lifestyle and belief.

CASE STUDY

Patrick works in an inner city school close to an area with a significant Chinese population. There are no Chinese children in the school, but Patrick feels that it is important that the children in his Reception class learn something about this community which is almost on the school's doorstep. As the Chinese New Year is approaching, Patrick decides to use this as the basis of an introduction to Chinese customs and lifestyle. His only contact with the community is his visits to the Chinese restaurant at the end of the road.

One day after school he visits the restaurant and strikes up a conversation with the owner. He explains his desire to introduce the children to the Chinese community and the owner is delighted to be involved. Together they plan a series of activities for the children. The restaurant owner, Mr Chan arranges to come into school to do some cooking with the children. He also brings in some artefacts associated with New Year – a calendar, some lucky money envelopes, some greetings cards. The children make fortune cookies, writing their own fortunes to put inside. They construct a huge Chinese dragon out of large cardboard boxes. Their work culminates with a celebratory meal, cooked by themselves and attended by Mr Chan and some of his staff.

Communication, language and literacy

RE contributes to children's communication development through aspects such as: listening with enjoyment, responding to stories, extending their vocabulary, using language to imagine and create roles and experiences, using talk to organise and clarify thinking, and re-telling narratives. Chapter 4 offers a detailed discussion of the role of story in RE across all ages and we recommend the 'A Gift to the Child' material (Grimmitt et al., 1991 and 2006) which provides a pedagogy for Early Years linking engagement with explicitly religious stories and artefacts with the experiences of particular young children. Stories from religion which particularly resonate with the experience of Foundation Stage include:

- Jesus' parables of the lost sheep and the lost coin (Christian);
- Rama and Sita, Ganesh, boyhood of Krishna (Hindu);
- The revelation to Muhammad (Muslim);
- Guru Nanak as a child (Sikh).

It is also important to recognise the significance of speaking and listening in RE. Some of the conversations may be spontaneous; you will need to seize the opportunities.

PRACTICAL TASK PRACTICAL TASK PRACTICAL TASK PRACTICAL TASK PRACTICAL TASK

Read the following extract and consider the questions that follow.

Sophie's Nursery class are helping to develop a wild-life area in the school grounds. As part of their 'speaking and listening' curriculum, Sophie wants them to talk about their relationship to the natural world, and in particular their views about the treatment of animals. As the children are clearing some ground, she is ready to pick up on conversation that might lead to a discussion. Sarah finds a dead bee:

Sarah: *Ah! A bee!* (She jumps away)

Sophie: *What's wrong?*

Sarah: *A bee, I don't like bees.*

David: *Ha! It's dead, silly.*

Sophie: *Why don't you like bees?*

Sarah: *'Cos they sting you.*

David: *They only sting you if you make them angry.*

Sophie: *Is that right?*

Jonathon: *Yes it's true, my mum said.*

Sophie: *What shall we do with it now?*

Sarah: *Throw it away!*

David: *No, let's bury it.*

Sophie: *Why should we bury it?*

David: *'Cos then it can go to heaven.*

Jonathon: *Bees don't go to heaven!*

Sophie: *Why not?*

Jonathon: *'Cos only people go.*

Sarah: *No, that's not right. My cat went to heaven.*

- How does Sophie make use of the event to develop the children's speaking and listening skills?
- How does she know they are listening to each other?
- What does she learn about the children's knowledge and understanding?
- What does she learn about their beliefs and values?
- How could Sophie use this conversation to develop the skills of other children in the class?

We need also to be aware of our own use of language when working in RE. The Standards remind us that teachers should: *adapt their language to suit the learners they teach, introducing new ideas and concepts clearly, and using explanations, questions, discussions and plenaries effectively* Q25c.

Creative development

RE contributes to this area by offering children opportunities to:

- use their imagination in art, design, music, dance, imaginative play, role play and stories;
- respond to experiences and express and communicate ideas;
- respond in a variety of ways to what they see, hear, smell, touch and feel.

The following are ideas for creative development through RE:

- music composition linked to the telling of a religious story. Give children percussion instruments to use at an appropriate moment or to accompany certain characters in a story;
- art work emerging from discussion of feelings; using art to communicate their beliefs about the world, about life;
- construction focusing on religious buildings, or religious artefacts;
- designing of clothes for special occasions;
- exploring pattern, for example in mendhi designs or Islamic designs;
- lots of opportunities for structured play connected with religious rituals and stories (see below).

Identifying themes and topics for RE

If we bring together children's experiences of religion, the aims of RE and the Early Years Foundation Stage curriculum, we begin to identify some of the key themes that will inform our planning and practice in the classroom. Furthermore, the QCA National Framework for RE states that:

During the Foundation Stage, children may begin to explore the world of religion in terms of special people, books, times, places and objects and by visiting places of worship. They may listen to and talk about stories. They may be introduced to religious words and use their senses in exploring religions and beliefs, practices and forms of expression. They reflect on their own feelings and experiences. They use their imagination and curiosity to develop their appreciation and wonder of the world in which they live. (QCA, 2004, p21)

Identity and belonging

This theme is an important one, both in terms of RE and for children's general development. There are lots of topics that can be explored under this umbrella term including the following.

- The importance of names
- Who am I?
- Caring for babies
- Naming/welcoming ceremonies, e.g. baptism
- My family
- Growing up
- What it means to belong
- Belonging in a Jewish family, Christian family, Sikhism, etc.

Example of a concept map on 'Babies'
In Figure 1 you can see the initial thoughts and ideas of a teacher as she began to explore the topic of 'Babies'. She thought as widely as she could, although she knew that she would not have time to explore every aspect. The time of year is obviously significant here. If she is teaching the unit in the Autumn, it would make sense to pursue the 'Jesus as a baby' aspect. If, however, it was to be taught in Spring, then the new life, Easter or baptism angle might be explored. Note that this level of planning fulfils the requirements of QTS Standards (Q22): *Plan for progression across the age and ability range for which they are trained, designing effective learning sequences within lessons and across series of lessons and demonstrating secure subject/curriculum knowledge.*

Example of using a story to explore 'Who am I?'
In the plan below, a children's picture book is used to explore the notion of identity and belonging. Mick Inkpen's story tells of a cloth cat which is left abandoned in a house, believing its name to be 'Nothing'. Nothing embarks on a journey to discover who he is, and where he belongs. As he meets different creatures he begins to remember who he is, eventually being reunited with his family.

Story: *Nothing* by Mick Inkpen
Area of learning: Personal Social and Emotional Development
Teacher-led activity: Yes
Number of children: 10
Age of children: 4–5 years
Time: 9.30–10.00 Monday to Friday

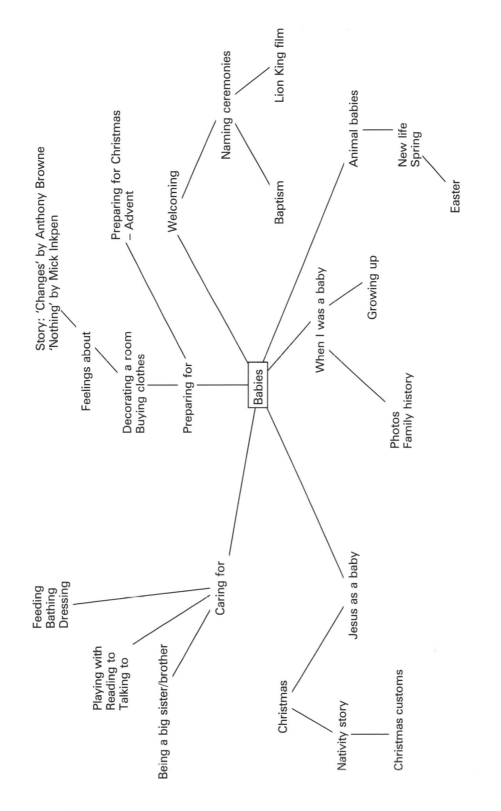

Figure 1 Concept map on babies

Day	Story section	Questions for discussion
Monday	1. Introduce the story – that it's about a toy who doesn't know who he is.	How did we get our names? What must it be like to think you are 'Nothing'? How do you think Nothing feels?
	2. Read: the introduction and up to page 6: Nothing finds himself abandoned.	Have we ever felt lost or alone? How did it feel?
Tuesday	1. Ask the children what happened to Nothing yesterday.	Who do you think the mouse reminded Nothing of? How do you think he feels leaving the attic and going into the world? Do you ever go anywhere on your own?
	2. Read pages 7–12: Nothing meets the mouse and leaves the attic.	
Wednesday	1. Ask the children what happened to Nothing yesterday.	What do the animals remind Nothing of? How is he the same or different to the animals he meets?
	2. Read pages 13–16: Nothing meets other creatures on his journey.	How are we similar/different from each other?
Thursday	1. Ask the children what has happened to Nothing up to now.	Why does the cat take Nothing on a journey? Have you ever been on a big journey? What was it like?
	2. Read pages 17–22: Nothing meets the cat.	How did you feel?
Friday	1. Ask the children where Nothing was when they last heard the story.	How do you think Nothing feels at the end of the story? How do you think the family feels? If you have ever been lost, how did you feel when you were found again? Have you ever lost something, how did it feel?
	2. Read pages 23 to the end: Nothing is reunited with his family.	

The discussion work that arises from this story has explicit connections with religious themes such as identity, belonging, relationship to others, special journeys (pilgrimage), separation and reconciliation. We would not want to follow all of these up at one time, but selecting one or two can help us to prepare children for their more explicit RE work later in the school.

Special places

There are a variety of places that can be identified as 'special' within a religious context. As usual we can begin with the children exploring the places that are special to them. What is important is that we not only ask children which places are special to them, but begin to encourage them to articulate WHY it is special.

PRACTICAL TASK PRACTICAL TASK PRACTICAL TASK PRACTICAL TASK PRACTICAL TASK

Imagine that you wish to ask a group of 3- and 4-year-olds to think about somewhere that is special to them. You might begin by telling them somewhere that is special to you, or you might read them a story about a child's special place. You could also use a puppet or soft toy, for which you have made a 'special place', and explain why it is special to them.

Having given the children a model of why places might be special, you then ask them to consider their own special places. It is important to anticipate their answers so that you consider how a very young child might respond to such a question. What answers do you think you might receive? What places might be special to young children and why? Make a list of possible responses.

From considering their own special places and sharing this with their classmates, children can move on to look at other people's 'special places'. These could include:

- other people's homes (see classroom suggestion below);
- places for worship, e.g. church, synagogue, home, temple.

Special times

Work in this area might include exploring the times that the children think of as special or important. They might think of birthdays, holidays, family occasions, festival times. Saturday might be special if that's the only day of the week on which they see their father. Their understanding of what makes a day or an occasion special can then be applied to religious days and times – Shabbat, Eid, a Christening, a wedding. Festivals are one of the most popular ways of exploring religion with children. Chapter 3 explores festivals, including linking them to other areas of the curriculum.

Other aspects of religions to explore

Special objects
What things are special to us and why?

- Holy books – Bible, Qur'an, Guru Granth Sahib (see also Chapter 4 on RE and Literature).
- Artefacts – cross, puja tray, Qur'an stand, rosary beads (see also Chapter 2).

Special people and relationships
Which people are special to us and why?

- Religious leaders – rabbi, priest, imam.
- Founders of faith – Jesus, the prophet Muhammad, Guru Nanak.

Lifestyle and food
- How do we know how to live?
- How do we know what we need to do?
- What foods do we eat and why?
- What foods don't we eat and why?
- Why do we have particular food on special occasions?
- What clothes do we wear and when?

Structured play and RE

Structured play gives children the opportunity to enter into and 'play' with knowledge they acquire through first hand experience, books, television and other information from teachers. Such play areas give children the opportunities to consolidate the knowledge and perhaps more importantly make sense of it in terms of their own understanding of the world. Structured play may be small-world play where the children in effect act as ' god' as they manipulate characters, or role-play where they are a participant actor.

Small world play

Dolls' houses can be decorated for festivals. Cloth synagogues and other artefacts can be purchased from Articles of Faith and/or you can turn other toys into characters to be used in re-enactments of stories.

CASE STUDY

Katy, a Reception class teacher, scoured charity shops for discarded Action Man dolls. She dressed them up in simple cloths and put them near the water tray. The children had great fun playing at John the Baptist baptising Jesus. In their play they were consolidating the story.

A structured role-play area

Setting up the home

Start with a story of a particular child of the relevant faith (see Chapter 2: Starting with the particular) and then set up the home from there. Parents may be a useful source of materials. Show children DVD clips and/or photos woven into a story, of things that might happen in the home. This can provide a model and inspiration for their play.

CASE STUDY:
UZMAH'S HOME

Figure of Uzmah: This play area has been deliberately set up as a home in which children can play at being part of the family or the guests. In calling it Uzmah's home there is a deliberate distancing. Children will recognise some items in the home as things which belong also in their homes and others which are to do with Uzmah's cultural and religious background. Making the home that of one individual, prevents the overgeneralisation implicit in making it a 'Muslim' home. A cardboard cut out of Uzmah is placed near the entrance. She wears a shalwar-kameez, a long dress and baggy pants, popular among Muslims from the Indian sub-continent. Muslim dress code decrees that all parts of the body should be covered in loose clothing when a person is outside the home. Many Muslim women, but not all, wear the hijab, a head-covering, when outside the home.

Moon: The Islamic calendar is a lunar one based on the cycle of the moon. A new moon will mark the beginning of the holy month of Ramadan, during which time Muslims fast from sunrise to sunset. A new crescent moon will also signify the end of Ramadan and the start of the Eid ul-Fitr celebrations. When Ramadan falls in the winter months so that the moon appears before children's bedtime, they can be given looking

---

at the moon and remembering or drawing its shape as a regular homework task, weather permitting (note the link to Knowledge and Understanding of the World).

Qur'an and Qur'an stand: The Qur'an (a real one isn't used) is always wrapped in a cloth when not in use, and kept on a high shelf above all other words as a mark of respect for the words, which are believed to be the direct words of God.

Wall decorations: Arabic calligraphy and pictures of Mecca often adorn Muslim homes. This shows the importance of the faith. Many, though not all Muslims, will not have photographs on display at all because of a prohibition on depicting the faces of living creatures. Others see this prohibition as only belonging to the mosque.

Prayer mat and prayer times: Muslims pray five times a day in line with the position of the sun rather than the clock, i.e. if the sun rises earlier the pre-dawn prayers are earlier. Prayer times are often displayed. A prayer mat is used to make a clean place to pray. Prayer is always done facing towards the direction of Mecca.

Eid cards: Cards are sent to wish people a happy Eid. Children can make their own cards to send to Uzmah and from her family (note the link to literacy).

Bowls of fruit and box of dates: The Ramadan fast is usually broken with dates. There is a particular point of having fresh fruit during Ramadan. There is a special effort to decorate the home with flowers during the month.

Zakatbox: Money is collected for charity during Ramadan.

Chapatties: Chapatties can be deliberately made out of rough cardboard, being symbolic of chapatties rather than play replicas. The ability to make and handle symbols is fundamental to a wide range of learning, including RE. Children have a natural capacity for symbolic play; this needs nourishing.

Dressing up box: Hats, scarves and shalwar-kameez.

Reading material – magazines, newspapers, catalogues, recipe books, etc.: The material could be in a mixture of Indian languages and English.

Books by the child's bed: Books by the cot or bed in a structured play area encourage children to 'read' to the 'baby' in the bed. Here we might have a range of books which include stories of two of the prophets that Islam shares with Christianity and Judaism, Noah and Moses. It is also possible to obtain children's versions of stories from Islam.

Developing play in the area

The more children can be involved in making such an area better, even if it is only to decide with you what should go into the house after an initial lesson on growing up in a Muslim family.

New items can be added or changed on a regular basis; e.g. the moon will be changed as Eid approaches. During Eid a meal will be laid out on the floor, as it is customary among many Muslims from the Indian sub-continent to sit on the floor to eat. Cutlery is not normally used.

If the play area is set up during Hannukah and Christmas then the point can be made that Muslims will send cards to their Jewish and Christian friends. Many Muslims also have a special meal on Christmas day because they view Jesus (Isa) as a prophet.

Adults in role

Generally it is preferable to let children be in charge, with an adult responding to their play. However there is some opportunity for adult role-play:

- postman/woman arriving with a recorded parcel;
- neighbour asking for an inconveniently parked car to be moved;
- washing machine repair person;
- family or friend visitor.

An alternative approach

An alternative approach is to leave the creation of the space entirely to children. Props for play are available for children, but they have the freedom to respond to the day's story, whether fiction or non-fiction, as they desire. Here the play truly belongs to the children.

Thus instead of setting out the play area the teacher ensures that there are the props available for the children to respond to the story, e.g. baggy pants, tops and head scarves in the dressing-up box, a mat which could be used as a prayer mat, picture books, perhaps a picture of Mecca, although children could draw their own.

Using the role-play area in this way can be done for any of the world religions.

Some other structured play areas with a cultural/religious dimension

Other ideas for a structured play area include:

- shop selling Muslim items, e.g. prayer mats, beads, Qur'ans, etc.;
- newsagency – seasonal cards, cards associated with rites of passage, e.g. birth, bar mitzvah, weddings, death, passing driving test; newspapers and magazines from different cultures;
- cake shops – shapes linked to the seasons, celebration cakes;
- the Christmas story – crib with straw, crowns, soft toy animals, tea towels for shepherds, inn-keeper's registration book, passports;
- a church (or other place of worship) – stained glass windows with the life of Jesus, lectern for Bible, bowl as font, hymn books, candlesticks, hymn numbers board, piece of cloth for a cape.

PRACTICAL TASK PRACTICAL TASK PRACTICAL TASK PRACTICAL TASK PRACTICAL TASK

Imagine you are planning to use the role-play area as a home from a different religion. What items would you put into the area? Use information in the Appendix as a start.

Conclusion

The skilled Foundation teacher in RE is one who both responds to the children and broadens their horizons. Effectively there is a continuing dynamic of the teacher responding to the children's responses. The stimulus may have been initiated by a child, or the teacher may have contributed it in the form of an image or story. This chapter has given you guidance towards becoming that skilled teacher.

A SUMMARY OF **KEY POINTS**

In this chapter we have explored:

> the importance of integrating RE into the Early Years curriculum in a meaningful way;

> the different ways in which RE can be incorporated into the Early Years curriculum;

> the importance of recognising and providing for children's level of development and their previous experiences both inside and out of school;

> how to make use of a wide range of activities and resources which will engage and challenge the children;

> how to create opportunities for play in RE.

MOVING *ON* > > > > > > **MOVING** *ON* > > > > > > **MOVING** *ON*

RE can be explored within many areas of the Early Years Foundation Stage curriculum. Examine the guidance for the curriculum and make a note of possible RE links.

8
Planning in RE

Chapter objectives

By the end of this chapter you will:

- **have an overview of the planning process in RE, including long-, medium- and short-term planning;**
- **recognise how RE principles and pedagogy explored in earlier chapters feed into the planning process;**
- **understand how to use differentiation in response to children's learning needs in RE;**
- **recognise the importance of continuity and progression in RE.**

This chapter addresses the following Standards for QTS: **Q3b, Q10, Q15, Q17, Q18, Q19, Q22, Q23, Q24, Q25**

Introduction

Anyone aiming to be an effective teacher recognises the value of careful planning. Whatever the subject, planning is vital in order to:

- identify what learning needs to take place;
- establish what knowledge the teacher needs to have;
- identify the resources that will be required;
- select the best teaching and learning strategies;
- select the best organisational strategies;
- anticipate the responses of the children;
- consider the needs of individual children;
- consider how the teacher will know if learning has taken place.

The QTS Standards for teachers remind us that we must:

> have a knowledge and understanding of a range of teaching, learning and behaviour management strategies and know how to use and adapt them, including how to personalise learning and provide opportunities for all learners to achieve their potential. (Q10)

Our thinking about such knowledge and understanding needs to be evident in our plans and careful planning for it is essential in RE if we are both to make it relevant to the children and handle complex issues in a meaningful way.

The planning process is usually described as including three stages: long-term, medium-term and short-term. In the sections below this process is described in relation to RE, highlighting the different considerations that need to be addressed at each stage of the process.

Long-term planning in RE

The process begins at a school level, in which the needs and expectations of the school community are addressed. In Chapter 1 we saw that whole school RE planning begins with recognising the status of the school to identify which syllabus needs to be followed (see Chapter 1 and Standards Q3 and Q15).

Using the relevant syllabus, the school will then begin to identify its own priorities in relation to the children it serves, the resources available and its wider school policies and philosophy. The syllabus will usually give detailed suggestions as to the content that might be covered and the school may also use the National Framework for RE (QCA, 2004) as an additional resource.

At this stage a whole-school approach is needed in order to:

- ensure that all teachers know and understand the policy for RE;
- enable the school to communicate their policy for RE to parents and children;
- decide upon how RE will be organised in the curriculum;
- decide which religions would be mainly studied;
- ensure a coherent approach throughout the school;
- identify the progression in learning across age groups.

PRACTICAL TASK PRACTICAL TASK PRACTICAL TASK PRACTICAL TASK PRACTICAL TASK

Think about a school that you have worked in and consider these questions:

- Did you see a policy for RE?
- Which syllabus was the school using?
- How was RE timetabled?
- How was it organised?
- What evidence of RE was there around school?
- What resources were available for RE?
- Were there schemes of work available for each year group?

Alongside the requirements of the relevant syllabus, the school also needs to consider the needs of the children it is providing RE for. The backgrounds of the children will guide the school in deciding what is the most appropriate approach to RE (see Standard Q18). It will also help the school to choose which religions should be focused on. Remember there is no requirement for children to study all six world religions (see Chapter 1).

REFLECTIVE TASK

Having read the information above, read the OFSTED-type descriptions of two schools below and consider/discuss the questions that follow.

School 1

Wellington Road Primary School is situated to the south of Peppleton city centre in an area of high unemployment. There are 363 pupils on roll. Children enter the school with lower than average ability levels. Over half are eligible for free school meals. The majority of children are of minority ethnic heritage, almost two-thirds of whom are learning English as an additional language. The proportion of children entering or leaving the school in different year groups is high. Some children are new to the UK.

School 2

Peppleton Church of England School is a Voluntary Aided school in south Peppleton. The children's backgrounds are mostly socially and economically above the average. The proportion of children with special educational needs is low. The majority of children are white British, but the number of children from minority ethnic backgrounds is above the national average. Few children come from families where English is not the first language. Children join the school with above-average skills.

- What features do you think are significant for the teaching of RE at each school?
- In what ways might those features contribute towards the school's planning for RE?
- Would the type of RE that the children receive be different in each school? Why?

The next stage of the process is for the school to plan which RE topics will be studied by children in the different year groups and how it will be included in the weekly timetable. Many schools adopt a cross-curricular approach in which RE is included within a theme (see Chapter 1). Other schools choose to do an RE topic as their main topic for a half term, while others simply teach one or two lessons of RE a week.

Below is an example of how one of the schools featured above planned its RE from the Nursery to Year 6.

CASE STUDY:
RE AT WELLINGTON ROAD PRIMARY SCHOOL

Using the Local Agreed Syllabus as a basis, the staff at Wellington Road School decided to update their approach to RE to meet the needs of their children more closely. They decided to focus on two religions at Key Stage 1 and three religions at Key Stage 2.

Whole school RE Plan for Wellington Road Primary School

	Autumn 1	Autumn 2	Spring 1	Spring 2	Summer 1	Summer 2
EYFS	Me and my family	Happy times	No RE	New life	Homes	No RE
Year 1	Family celebrations	Celebrating Eid*	Who was Muhammad?	New beginnings	No RE	Belonging
Year 2	Who was Jesus?	How do Christians celebrate Christmas?	Caring for the world	Stories from Islam	Who lives around here?	The Church
Year 3	Stories from Christianity	Celebrating Diwali	At home with a Hindu family	Easter customs	The Qur'an	At home with a Muslim family
Year 4	Journeys	Introducing the Bible	The Mosque	Being a Christian	Religion in our area	Caring for others

Year 5	Pilgrimage in Islam	The meaning of Christmas	Stories from Hinduism	The meaning of Easter	Living as a Muslim	Creation
Year 6	Questions and Answers	Christmas around the world	The Hindu Temple (Mandir)	Rules and respon-sibility	Ideas about God	Growing up in religion
		* This topic may move to match the date of Eid ul-Fitr				

It can be seen from Wellington Road's plans that themes are revisited as the children go through the school, building on their previous learning. This ensures progression and development (see below) and ensures that their RE curriculum has coherence across their primary experience.

Medium-term planning in RE

Once the whole-school long-term plan is in place, each teacher can begin to plan how to deliver each topic across the year. Most RE topics lend themselves to a cross-curricular approach and so teachers may look for links with other areas of the curriculum. For example, the Year 4 RE topic 'Journeys', above, has obvious links with geography, allowing the children to explore religious journeys, but also to fulfil some geographical learning objectives.

It is common for teachers to plan a half-term ahead – approximately 6–7 weeks. The teacher needs to decide how much curriculum time can be devoted to RE over this time. Clearly, far more can be done in three hours per week than one and so this will indicate how much can RE can be planned.

Teachers will then develop their Scheme of Work or Unit Plan for each RE topic. They will consider the main things they want the children to learn, the resources they will need and the teaching strategies they will use.

Selecting learning objectives

Selecting objectives for the unit will involve consideration of three things:

1   the children's previous learning related to the topic;
2   the children's backgrounds and experiences;
3   the aims of the relevant syllabus.

It is important to involve the children as much as possible in all aspects of planning in order to give them responsibility for their learning and identify where their interests lie. It also helps teachers to find out what the children already know and what they would like to find out.

CASE STUDY

At the end of each term John involves his Year 4 class in planning for the RE topic they will be covering after the school holiday. At the end of the first Autumn term he tells the children that after the break they will be looking at Diwali as part of the Hindu tradition. He splits the class into small groups and asks them to write down everything they know about Diwali. There are several Hindu children in the class who willingly share their knowledge with their non-Hindu group members.

In the discussion that follows, John discovers that there is a considerable amount of knowledge shared by both the Hindu and non-Hindu children. They know the main details of the story of Rama and Sita, and that lights are associated with the festival. John then asks each group to think of what else they would like to know about Diwali, and to write a list. Again, the groups settle quickly to the task.

John gathers the class together to compile a class list. He then asks the class to select the most useful questions. The children recognise that some questions might be difficult to find out about, such as 'What was Rama and Sita's second name?'. Some questions are then prioritised as areas for investigation. The class agree on five main questions:

- Why is Diwali important to Hindus?
- Do all Hindus celebrate Diwali?
- Why do Sikhs celebrate Diwali too?
- How is Diwali celebrated in India?
- Did the story of Rama and Sita actually happen?

Finally, John asks the class how they might begin to find out about these aspects of Diwali. They come up with the following suggestions.

- Use the internet.
- Ask parents and family.
- Find books on Diwali.
- Visit the local Mandir (temple).

John is able to use the children's suggestions to plan their work after the holiday.

From consideration of the children's prior experiences and learning needs, a set of learning objectives for the unit can be generated. Syllabuses and the National Framework for RE can be useful resources for identifying suitable objectives.

In the past, OFSTED has been critical of RE that focuses only on what knowledge the children will be developing. RE is about much more than knowledge; it needs to address under-standing, values, attitudes and skills.

When planning RE, teachers should ask themselves the following questions which address three main aspects of RE:

1 What knowledge and understanding of the topic do I want children to gain?
2 What values and attitudes do I want them to develop?
3 What skills do I want them to develop?

These aspects are usually brought together in the two QCA Attainment Targets for RE: AT1 Learning about Religion and AT2 Learning from Religion (see Chapter 1 for further detail about the QCA Attainment Targets).

Knowledge and Understanding involves children exploring and investigating aspects of different religious traditions such as beliefs, practices, festivals, leaders, lifestyle, stories and so on. The kinds of values and attitudes that RE involves include: self-awareness, open-mindedness, enquiry, curiosity, response, sensitivity, tolerance, respectfulness and appreciation. The skills which children might develop through RE include those of observation, listening, investigation, communication, reflection, analysis, empathy and evaluation.

PRACTICAL TASK PRACTICAL TASK PRACTICAL TASK PRACTICAL TASK PRACTICAL TASK

From discussion with the children about Diwali, John generated 4 unit aims which he could develop into specific learning opportunities:

By the end of the unit the children will:

- understand the meaning and significance of Diwali for Hindus;
- know some of the ways that Diwali is celebrated in different places.;
- have reflected on the nature of a religious story;
- be able to articulate how Diwali helps explain human experience.

Can you match John's unit aims to the three aspects above and the relevant QCA Attainment Targets?

Selecting appropriate learning opportunities

Once unit aims are established, consideration of what activities the children will be involved in can take place. Clearly we would want activities to engage the children, and be designed to help them towards the learning objectives (see section on personalised learning below).

A range of activities needs to be planned to take account of children's learning needs and preferences. Many activities will automatically draw on other curriculum subjects such as English and literacy, art and design (see Standards Q17 and Q23).

Identifying resources

Once activities are chosen, the implications for resources have to be considered. The quality of any RE work will obviously depend on the range of resources available to the teacher. For each stage of the unit, the teacher needs to consider which ones will best support the children's learning. As well as general school equipment, other specific items such as films, music, religious artefacts, visitors and visits may be useful. Religious artefacts can be sourced from specialist shops, via the internet and from local faith communities and shops. It may also be possible to borrow items from families. (See Chapter 2 on the use and care of religious artefacts.) It is important too to establish links with local communities in order to provide opportunities for children to meet members of faith traditions and to visit relevant places. The children's parents are obviously one source, and they might also be able to contact community religious leaders who can help. (See Chapter 2 on using visits in RE.)

Another very important resource is the teacher's own background knowledge. Clearly, not everyone is going to be an expert in six world religions, but it is important to spend time researching a specific topic so that you have an adult understanding of the topic. There are many valuable books on religions available and the internet of course is becoming an ever more valuable resource. Focused research is vital, you do not need to know everything there is to know about each religion, just add to your knowledge a little at a time. For example, research a particular aspect, such as how a Jewish family might observe Shabbat (the Sabbath).

Homework

There are lots of valuable activities that children can do as homework, including individual research, responding to tasks set or reflecting on work done in school (Standard Q24).

PRACTICAL TASK PRACTICAL TASK PRACTICAL TASK PRACTICAL TASK PRACTICAL TASK

You are teaching 'How do Christians celebrate Christmas?' with a Year 2 class. You want them to consider how Christians in different places and at different times have celebrated Christmas. You want them to research in their own time – what task could you set them? What guidance would you give? Remember that some children will be from worshipping Christian families and others not. Design the task.

Assessing learning and evaluating the unit

The final part of medium-term planning is thinking about how you will know if your teaching is effective. To this end, you need to consider what criteria you will use for evaluating the success of the unit. One criterion must be whether the children have learned anything. You must plan how you will assess the children's learning in a meaningful way that will help you to identify what progress they have made, what misconceptions they might have and what they need to do next (see Chapter 9 on assessment).

CASE STUDY

On pages 101–102 is a medium-term unit plan for a Year 4 unit on 'Journeys' (see Whole-School Plan for Wellington Road School above).

PRACTICAL TASK PRACTICAL TASK PRACTICAL TASK PRACTICAL TASK PRACTICAL TASK

Use the unit planner on page 103 to develop the topic of Questions and Answers for a Year 6 class.

Short-term lesson planning in RE

The final level of planning is short-term, usually thought of as lesson or activity plans. These are developed from the medium-term unit plan and are specific to each lesson or activity. The purpose of the lesson plan is to anticipate how the lesson will go. It is almost like a script which tracks all aspects of the lesson from beginning to end. The newer you are to teaching, the more detail you need in your plan. In an RE lesson plan certain features are crucial, for example, a good deal of RE work may be discussion-based. This means that organisation has to be considered, as well the strategies to get the discussion going and maintain it (see Standard Q25).

Title of Unit: Journeys	Year Group: 4	Date: Autumn 1

Aims of the unit:

By the end of the unit the children will:
- Understand the role of pilgrimage in religion (AT1)
- Be aware of the feelings associated with journeys (AT2)
- Understand the symbolic nature of journeying (AT1)

Previous learning: Many of the children have undertaken long journeys, both on their way to Britain and for holidays. One or two have been on Hajj.

Resources: World map, holiday brochures, video of Hajj, family photos, story of Muhammad's journey to Medina.

6 weeks x 1 hour lessons	Learning Objectives The children will:	Activity	Resources	Differentiation	Assessment Can the children:
Week 1: What is a journey?	– Examine and extend their understanding of 'journeying' – Appreciate the features and feelings associated with journeys	– Tell children about a journey you have made – your preparations, etc. – Discuss long journeys that we have been on, what was involved and how we felt at different stages – Plot contributions onto 3 stage image – before, during and after the journey	Book Paper Rulers Pencils	Support for those who may need help writing the 3 sections	– Retell some of their own journeys? – Identify contrasting feelings associated with journeys?
Week 2: Pilgrimage as a special journey	– Understand the role that pilgrimage plays in religion – Consider the feelings associated with pilgrimage – Develop their skills of co-operation	– Introduce the idea of special, holy journeys Gather any knowledge of religious journeys – Discuss how religious journeys are different from other ones – Children construct a group poster demonstrating their understanding of pilgrimage	Poster materials	– Friendship groups but ensuring that some in the group are confident writers/ artists – Establish roles in the group – Identify those who know about pilgrimage as 'experts'	– Articulate the importance of a religious journey? – Demonstrate their new knowledge? – Work as part of a team?

Week 3: Hajj in Islam I – Muhammad's journey	– Understand why Makkah is special to Muslims – Be able to identify and talk about some of the features of Hajj – Be able to articulate aspects of Hajj that they wish to learn more about	– Show video of young boy on Hajj – Ask the class to pick out main features – Discuss why each feature is significant. – Prepare questions for Mr Ahmad's visit	Video, pencils, paper, post cards	– Assist those who may need help constructing questions – Encourage those who can to think of more complex questions	– Explain importance of Makkah? – Generate thoughtful questions?
Week 4: Hajj in Islam II – a personal view	– Recognise the importance of Hajj for Muslims – Be able to demonstrate respect for Hajj in the Islamic faith	– Visit from Mr Ahmad to tell the children about his recent Hajj – Mr Ahmad describes his visit and shows photos – Children ask their prepared questions if they have not been answered		– Support for those who may need help reading out their questions – Make a list of any terms Mr Ahmad uses to explain/ask about later	– Ask questions in an appropriate manner? – Listen attentively? – Respond to answers? – Demonstrate their understanding?
Week 5: Hajj in Islam III – our responses	– Be able to express their understanding of Hajj creatively – Demonstrate an appreciation of the significance of Hajj – Work co-operatively as part of a team	– Children design a web page showing the significance of Hajj using images and sound	ICT suite	– Paired work ensuring at least one person is a confident writer	– Select appropriate resources? – Show originality? – Work co-operatively?
Week 6: Sharing our learning	– Be able to communicate their understanding to others – Demonstrate skills of selection, organisation and co-operation	– Group discussion of what should be included in a display – Design and construction of corridor display	Tables, boards, display materials, paper, artefacts, photos, etc.	– Encourage quieter group members to contribute by giving them key roles	– Summarise their learning? – Identify key features? – Appreciate what is needed in display?

Title of Unit: Questions and Answers	Year Group: 6		Date: Autumn 1		
Aims of the unit:	By the end of the unit the children will: recognise different kinds of questions (AT1) understand that some questions can only be answered by faith (AT1) respect the right of people to have different answers to ultimate questions (AT2) be able to articulate their own answers to ultimate questions (AT2)				
Previous learning:	Throughout their RE lessons the children have become familiar with asking questions. They are aware that some questions are harder to answer than others				
Resources:					
6 weeks x 1 hour lessons	**Learning Objectives**	**Activity**	**Resources**	**Different-iation**	**Assessment**
Week 1:					
Week 2:					
Week 3:					
Week 4:					
Week 5:					
Week 6:					

There are many different ways of constructing a lesson plan. Many teachers use an electronic pro-forma containing a grid which can be used for different lessons. Whichever layout teachers prefer, all lessons should contain elements of the following.

Learning objectives

Like the overall unit objectives, lesson objectives should relate to the knowledge and understanding, the attitudes, skills and values associated with RE, that it is hoped the children will develop during the lesson. It is important to clarify initially what kind of a lesson it is to be. Is it an introduction to a new topic, consolidation or extension of previous learning, or is it one where children will apply new knowledge or skills?

Whichever type it is, it is crucial that the learning objectives are precise and can be achieved during the lesson. Too often, teachers try to cover too much in an RE lesson. It is better to have a narrow focus that leads to deeper understanding, than too wide a focus that leads to superficiality. For example, 'The children will learn about Islam' is far too broad and vague. A better one would be, 'The children will be able to retell the story of Muhammad's journey to Medina'.

Previous learning

If the lesson is the first one in a topic, then previous learning will refer back to:

- any RE work they have done before that will help them understand this topic;
- any broader knowledge and/or skills that the children may have from other subjects;
- any work they have done on this topic before, i.e. if they are re-visiting a topic;
- any knowledge/skills/experiences the children have had outside school which might help them understand the topic.

If the lesson develops the topic, then previous learning will include reference to the previous lesson and how this prepared them for the current lesson.

Lesson structure and content

It is helpful to consider a lesson as a series of activities so that you break the session down into segments. This enables you to consider each stage of the lesson to address progression and to identify what the children's experience will look like. Remember that the younger the child, the shorter each segment of the lesson is likely to be if you are to keep the child engaged and keep track of their responses and achievements.

Many teachers tend to plan a lesson in three main segments – beginning, middle and end. However, you may find that you need to divide the lesson further, perhaps thinking in 10-minute segments. You would ask yourself 'What will the children and I be doing for the next 10 minutes?' It is also helpful to write estimated timings on your plan to help you manage the time effectively.

Creativity is key to effective teaching and learning in RE (see Chapters 2 and 3). The activities we provide for the children must be designed to give them a positive experience of RE that makes it interesting and relevant. Children need to be active in their own learning, taking responsibility for it and feeling involved in the subject. You will also want to consider the best way to approach world religions (see Chapter 2) and how to incorporate Thinking Skills (see Chapter 5).

Effective beginnings

If the lesson is an introductory one, then the first part of it will involve you finding out what do they know already. If the lesson builds on a previous one, then you will be checking what the class has remembered from last time. Traditionally this process involves the teacher asking questions to the whole class. One problem with this technique is that generally only a few children take part, leaving the teacher unsure as to how widely knowledge and understanding is shared. A further difficulty lies in matching questions to the needs of the children, calling for differentiated questioning.

It is important to help children to remember their previous learning and experiences. Offering them 'thinking time' and/or giving them opportunity to share their thoughts with a neighbour before offering an answer is valuable. Another strategy might be to display questions, an object or an image about prior learning, to trigger their memories. Puzzles and quizzes such as word searches can also be used.

CASE STUDY

Anne's Year 1 class had started to learn about Eid. In their second lesson, she wanted to see what they had remembered from the week before. Anne told the children she was going to show them some pictures of work they had done last week. She asked them to look at the pictures carefully and then talk to their neighbour about what the pictures showed. She displayed some images of families celebrating Eid on the interactive whiteboard. The children looked at the images and began to chat among themselves. When the images had finished Anne used the whiteboard to make a list of responses that the children made. From this she was able to see which aspects they had remembered, and also what misconceptions there were.

Many teachers also share the objectives for the lesson with the children. If this is done, we need to ensure that the objectives are presented in a way that children understand. They should also be made aware that although these objectives are focal ones, they may indeed learn other things during the time and we should encourage the children to share what they feel they have learned.

Engaging middles

In Chapter 2 the value of using a cross-curricular approach to teaching and learning in RE was explored. When planning the main input of the lesson, the teacher needs to consider a range of teaching and learning strategies in which the children are actively involved in their learning, have a degree of independence and make the most of their knowledge, skills, talents and interests. This section often forms the bulk of the lesson and may include elements of the following:

- introducing new learning;
- consolidating prior learning;
- developing or extending prior knowledge;
- applying knowledge, understanding or skills to new contexts.

For RE, this means drawing on a wide range of strategies and activities from across the curriculum which make good use of a range of appropriate resources to provide engaging learning opportunities for the children. Too often, RE suffers from an overemphasis on language, especially reading and writing. Sometimes this can inhibit children's responses, especially those with reading or writing difficulties, preventing them from developing their religious understanding.

Sometimes children are set tasks in RE which demand very little of them in terms of their knowledge, skills and experiences. Another trap to avoid is setting the children tasks that initially look like they are developing learning but in reality they are assessment tasks, for which children already need to have some knowledge. For example, look below at the two activities that different classes were given to do as part of their work on the local church. The first activity (A) shows part of a worksheet that children were given after their visit to the church. The second (B) shows a task that was written on the board.

A

Worksheet 3: Parts of a church

Last week we visited St Matthews church. The picture below is a picture of a church similar to St Matthews. At the bottom of the sheet are the names of different parts of the church. Draw a line from the names to the correct part of the church.

B

Which features of a church are important?

1 Look at the sketches and notes you made at the church last week.
2 Choose one feature of the church that interests you and draw it neatly into your book.
3 Using your notes and the books you have collected, explain what your feature is and how it is used by Christians when they visit the church.

REFLECTIVE TASK

In each activity

- What are the children being asked to do?
- What knowledge do they need to have?
- Where will they have got this knowledge from?
- How will the task help their understanding of what the church means to Christians?
- How engaging do you think the task would be for different members of the class?
- How demanding do you think it would be for different members of the class?
- How long do you think it would take the children to do this task?
- How much of it do you think they are likely to remember?

Satisfactory conclusions

Most teachers aim to have work completed by the end of a taught session, although some work may need to be continued at a later date, for example, if children are doing an extended piece of writing or some art work that has to be done in stages. A lesson conclusion may include a range of activities, often similar to the ones at the beginning. The children need to be given opportunity to share their learning, identify what they have enjoyed, report any difficulties they encountered and look forward to the next lesson in the unit.

CASE STUDY:
PLANTING SEEDS

All the children in Mrs Jones' Reception class had been taking it in turns to plant seeds in small trays as part of their work on 'New Life'. During the activity Mrs Jones had encouraged them to talk about what they were doing and its relationship to spring.

At the end of the morning all the children gathered on the carpet to review their work. Using pictures that Mrs Jones had drawn as prompts, the children shared with each other how they had gone about planting the seeds. They were able to explain that the seeds needed water and sunshine to grow. They estimated how long it would take them to flower and when this might happen. They knew that they had planted the seeds now because the weather was getting warmer outside. They agreed between them that they should measure them with a ruler each week to see how much they had grown.

Organisation and teacher's role (see also section 4 below)

Once different activities for each part of the lesson have been decided, it is necessary to consider how the learning context needs to be organised. Different parts of the lesson might be organised in different ways, the most common being: whole-class, group, pair and individual work. There are a range of factors that will influence these decisions, including:

- the type of activity set;
- the needs of individual children;
- the availability of resources;
- health and safety.

Another important aspect to consider is what role you will play during the lesson. To begin with, you need to be sure of the main teaching points you wish to communicate to the children. You then need to explore how you see yourself during different segments of the lesson. For example, you might be a guide, showing children how to access material, you might be one source of information, or a supervisor of activities. You might see yourself as a facilitator – setting up and managing the learning environment and chairing a discussion. You may also act as a model for the children, demonstrating how they might go about a task. You will certainly be involved in giving feedback to the children and you may need to support individuals in their learning. (See also below 'Further notes on the teacher's role'.)

REFLECTIVE TASK

Read the tasks that each teacher below is involved in. How would you describe their role?

- Amanda shows the class some Jewish artefacts and explains how they are used during Shabbat.
- Brenda is helping Katie to organise pictures into the correct order for the story.
- Carl has divided the class into two groups to discuss whether people should eat meat.
- Debbie asks her class what they want to know about the Qur'an.

- Ellen shows the class the poster that Davinder made about caring for the world. She explains why it is such a good poster.
- Fabia creates a Diwali card using the resources on the table and explains the task to the class.

Resources

Once the activities have been chosen for the lesson, the next stage is to identify what resources will be needed for each stage of the lesson. Obviously this will depend on what is immediately available in school, but if specific religious resources are required, time may be needed to buy, borrow or find these. If a visit to a place of worship is needed, this must be organised well ahead of time (see Chapter 2 on using visits in RE). Consideration of resources also includes thinking about which staff or adult support will be available and how much time is to be allocated to the lesson.

PRACTICAL TASK PRACTICAL TASK PRACTICAL TASK PRACTICAL TASK PRACTICAL TASK

Below is a list of resources that you might use for teaching about Judaism.

- If you are unfamiliar with any of the terms or items, research them.
- In the column next to the list make a list from another religion that you are familiar with.
- Consider where you might find each resource.

Resources for teaching Judaism	Resources for teaching
2 candlesticks for Shabbat Spice box Mezuzah Tefilin Tallith Hebrew Bible Model of a Torah scroll Yarmulka Hanukkiah Dreidle Matzah Hebrew prayer book Seder plate Star of David Greetings cards for festivals Bar mitzvah cards Wedding cards	

Please see Chapter 2 for further information on using artefacts in RE.

Personalised provision

All the lessons we plan for RE must be designed with the needs of our children in mind. Our lessons must be inclusive and reflect the diversity of the children we teach (see Standards Q10 and Q19).

If we use reading and writing as a vehicle for teaching RE then clearly we will need to consider the particular skills of each child in the class, just as we would for any other English task. The same is true for any skills-based activity we might provide. Children's special educational needs (SEN) must inform our planning. But are there other aspects of differentiation that we need to consider in RE?

In RE we need to consider the children, not just in terms of their academic levels, but also in terms of their religious, cultural, racial, social and moral backgrounds and perspectives. Children may have a great deal of contact with religion or none at all, and this will affect how they view and approach RE. Some children could be hostile to any talk of religion, or unsympathetic to religions different to their own. It is to be expected that the children's views will be influenced by their parents' and we need to be cautious about contradicting these. Of course, some parents will remove their children from RE (see Chapter 1), in which case our responsibility for their RE is also removed.

The teacher needs to be conscious of all of this in order to provide activities that are appropriate and that allow for a range of responses. Such consciousness is vital, particularly during debates and discussions, or around coverage of controversial issues (see below for further notes on the teacher's role).

Here are some examples of factors by which work might be differentiated.

- **Task**: Phil grouped the class according to their reading levels. Each group looked at a different story from Hinduism and had to produce a different response.
- **Support**: Eva circulated the classroom as the children worked, stopping briefly to check with specific children if they had understood the task and could read all the words.
- **Resources**: Bruce put 'writing frameworks' on each table, telling the children that they could use them to organise their story if they wished to.
- **Time**: Beth's dyslexia meant that she needed an extra 10 minutes to complete her diary account of her visit to Lourdes. She chose to do it while the other children were tidying up before lunch.
- **Outcome (expectations)**: Jean made a note on her plans of what she expected different children to be able to put in their 'Growing Up' book. She knew that Matthew, Hassim, Helen, Alistair and Georgie would be able to produce several pages of well-written, accurate work that showed a good understanding of their growing responsibilities. She also felt that Gavin, Penny and Michael would be able to draw some images of what they looked like at different ages. They should also be able to annotate those pictures with her help.

We also need to include a range of teaching and learning approaches which show awareness of children's learning styles and preferences, their own personal progress and targets, and the levels they are operating at.

Assessment and evaluation

The final question we need to consider when planning is 'How will I know what impact the lesson has had on the children?' This usually involves devising ways to find out what the children have learned and how they see their experience of the lesson (see Chapter 9 on assessment). Assessment need not be seen in terms of formal testing, but rather as an integral part of the learning process, which could take place during and/or after the activity. Any assessment needs to be based on the learning objectives for the lesson and teachers need to be sure that they know exactly what it is they are looking for in the children's work.

When we evaluate a lesson, we reflect back on each part of it to identify what worked well and was effective, and what changes we might need to make to improve a similar lesson in future. We can ask ourselves the following questions.

- How appropriate were the learning objectives?
- How coherent was the structure?
- How efficient was the organisation?
- How useful were the resources?
- How effectively did I support children's learning?
- How well did the activities match the learning objectives?
- How well did the activities match individual learning needs?
- How successful were the children in their learning?

From our answers to these questions we can begin to identify what changes we need to make in order to improve our practice.

Further notes on the teacher's role in RE

A lesson plan may contain much detail about what both the teacher and children will be doing during the lesson. However, teachers not only act as director of the learning, they also act as a model for the children and communicate many verbal and non-verbal messages in the way they manage the children and the learning environment. Because RE is an important and sensitive subject, teachers need to be aware of the message they are communicating as they teach. They also have a responsibility to protect children and establish a safe and secure environment where children feel confident to learn (see Standard Q30).

In RE, this means establishing rules for behaviour, especially in relation to discussion activities. Rules need to be established so that the children are aware that certain behaviour is expected, such as listening carefully to others, not interrupting, and so on. It is important that the children themselves discuss and generate such rules so that they have considered what is best for group discussion.

PRACTICAL TASK PRACTICAL TASK PRACTICAL TASK PRACTICAL TASK PRACTICAL TASK

Make a list of rules for discussion that would enable children to discuss RE topics safely and confidently. Remember that rules stated positively draw attention to the desired behaviour rather than undesirable behaviour, for example, 'we listen carefully when someone is speaking' is preferable to 'don't talk if it's not your turn'.

Not only are teachers responsible for establishing and maintaining an atmosphere conducive to learning, they also act as a model for the children. For RE this means that they should demonstrate the skills, values, qualities and attitudes that they are attempting to develop in the children. This means that they too should listen carefully when someone else is speaking. It also means they should challenge any contributions from the children that could be considered to be racist, sexist, stereotypical, homophobic or discriminatory in any way.

In order to demonstrate the active nature of RE and to encourage participation, teachers should also offer plenty of praise and encouragement, valuing all responses. Often RE will entail asking children 'open questions' to children that require their ideas, views, responses or thoughts. It is important here to make sure that children's contributions are not dismissed as being irrelevant or wrong. We want to demonstrate to the children that RE is about personal response to religious phenomena, not something that is either 'right' or 'wrong'.

Continuity and progression

We have seen in early chapters and in this one that a foundation stone of effective RE teaching is matching what we offer to the needs of the children. We must ensure at each stage of their development that we are building on what they have already done and experienced (see Standard Q22). This means that each time the children encounter an RE topic, they are offered something that extends, deepens and broadens their understanding. Too often in RE children are given the same kind of activities over and over again, resulting in a very narrow RE curriculum or a very superficial one in which they never develop their understanding.

Often it is the most popular RE topics that suffer from the worst treatment. Festivals are especially vulnerable to this because of their annual nature. It seems obvious to teach about festivals every year as they come round, but too often they are celebrated but not 'taught about'. If we take Christmas as a prime example, we find that in many schools a Nativity play is planned, children make Christmas cards and the school may be decorated. The story of the nativity may also be read to children and they may write letters to Father Christmas.

Below is an example of how Christmas might be explored across the age phases.

Year Group	RE topic on Christmas. 4 weeks, beginning the first week of Advent
EYFS	**Celebrating Birthdays** When is my birthday? – calendars Planning for the birth of a baby Planning a party Jesus' birthday
Year 1	**Special Times** My special times How do we celebrate special times? Why is Christmas a special time? The Christmas story
Year 2	**How Do Christian Children Celebrate Christmas?** A family Christmas Christmas carols Gifts and Giving Waiting for Father Christmas
Year 3	**The Church at Christmas** What is Advent? Visit from Father Johnson Christmas services Visit to the church
Year 4	**Christmas Customs** What can we learn from Christmas cards? Why do Christians decorate their homes at Christmas? Thinking of others at Christmas The symbolism of light
Year 5	**How Do We Know about Jesus?** Introducing the gospels Comparing the Gospel stories of the Nativity Symbolism in the Christmas story Jesus in Islam
Year 6	**The Significance of Jesus' Birth** Waiting for the Messiah Palestine at the time of Jesus' birth How Christmas is celebrated around the world Jesus as God Incarnate

Examples of lesson plans

Below are the plans for three lessons – for an Early Years Foundation Stage class, a Year 4 class and a Year 5 class. Each lesson demonstrates the central features of planning described above.

EYFS 1 lesson: Jesus' birthday

Date: 20th December **Time:** 25 min

Learning objectives:
By the end of the lesson the children will:
Understand that Christmas is a special time for Christians
Know a simple version of the nativity story
Understand that Christmas celebrates the birth of Jesus

Previous learning:
Lessons on birthdays, waiting for a baby, parties. Most of the children in the class celebrate Christmas.

Structure and content:
1. Gathered together in the reading area, talk about what we have been doing on babies, and birthdays. What can they remember? **5 min**
2. Tell the children we are going to hear about the birth of a very special baby. Can any of them guess who it is by looking at the stable? **2 min**
3. Tell the story using the nativity figures, allowing the children to identify characters and help tell the story where able. (Ms Garner to make notes of who contributes) **10 min**
4. Conclude the story by telling the children that Christmas is a special time for Christians because it's the time they think of Jesus being born – a bit like their own birthdays. **2 min**
5. Allow time for comments, questions and thoughts. **5 min+**

Resources:
Nativity set
Adults: Self and Ms Garner

Differentiation:
Encourage Julie, Ashraf, Ben, Phoebe and Callum to help tell the story.
Ms Garner to sit with Peter and Jenny.

Cross-curricular links:
Speaking and listening

Assessment:
Can the children:
Respond to the story by asking appropriate questions and making appropriate comments? (Ms Garner to make a note of who contributes)

Year 4 lesson: What can we learn from Christmas Cards?
Date: 1st December **Time:** 1 hour 15 min

Learning objectives:
By the end of the lesson the children will:
Recognise some of the symbols of Christmas
Understand significant aspects of the Christmas festival
Be able to express their understanding through art and design

Previous learning:
Lesson on Christmas customs in Britain.
Re-cap nativity story.

Structure and content:
Use word search to review learning on previous lessons.
Explain that we are going to look closer at the Christmas card custom to find out what we can learn about Christmas from them. **10 min**
Send to tables. In groups, sort through the Christmas cards on their tables and organise into groups of similar types. **10 min**
Ask for feedback – how did each group sort their cards? **10 min**
  Possible responses
  Religious/non-religious
  Father Christmas
  Animals, people
  Charity cards
  Colours
  Decorations
  Presents, etc.
Imagine you are a newly arrived alien from another planet. What would you think Christmas is about? In groups, jot down ideas. **10 min**
Each member of the group to choose a different feature and think of an explanation for that feature. Help each other where necessary. **10 min**
Consider which features you think really represent Christmas. Plan a Christmas card design in your ideas book. Discuss your plans with your group. **15 min**

Resources:
Christmas cards
Books about Christmas
Ideas books

Differentiation:
Mix groups to ensure a range of skills and knowledge.
Allow for a range of response in their written explanations.
Allow for a range of response in their designs for cards.

Cross-curricular links:
PSHE – working collaboratively

Assessment:
See learning objectives
Circulate groups to see who is contributing to discussion and how. Make notes.
Look at designs after lesson to see what understanding of the symbolism they show.

Year 5 lesson: Comparing the Gospel stories about Jesus' birth **Date:** 9th December **Time:** 45 min
Learning objectives: **By the end of the lesson the children will:** Understand that there are different versions of the story and why Understand that the stories reflect beliefs about Jesus Be able to articulate their own view about the stories
Previous learning: Introduction to the Gospel writers. Most children know a version of the nativity story.
Structure and Content: Quiz about the Gospels from previous lesson: – What 'g' means good news? – How many Gospels are there? – In which part of the Bible are the Gospels found? – Name the 4 Gospel writers. **5 min** Explain that we are going to look at the story of Jesus' birth as told by the Gospel writers. Distribute Matthew's version to half class and Luke's to the other half. Task is to underline the main features and events of the story. Work together around your table. (Ensure they cannot see other tables' version) **10 min** Bring class together and make a list on the board of features/events. As differences emerge, start another column. Why have they found different things? Draw attention to the two versions. Why should this be? Any suggestions? **10 min** Write a brief paragraph called 'The riddle of Jesus' birth'. Explain what you think about the riddle. **10 min** Plenary – volunteers to read out their paragraph **10 min**
Resources: Printed versions of Matthew and Luke nativity story Note pads
Differentiation: Ensure mixed groups to support each other in writing. Visit those children for whom writing more difficult. Scribe for Jodie.
Cross-curricular links: History – comparing sources PSHE – collaborative learning
Assessment: **Can the children:** Explain the differences between the stories in their paragraph?

Conclusion

Planning for RE is as important as in any other subject. Careful and imaginative planning will enable you to teach effectively to the benefit of the children and your own satisfaction.

A SUMMARY OF **KEY POINTS**

In this chapter we have explored:

> the complexity of the planning process in RE and the need for sufficient detail covering all aspects of the lesson;

> how syllabus and curriculum content needs to be balanced with consideration of the needs of the children;

> how careful planning helps to give the teacher confidence to understand the purpose of the lesson and how it contributes to children's learning in RE;

> the ways in which the needs of individual children can be met;

> the importance of anticipating children's responses and any potential issues or difficulties.

MOVING *ON* > > > > > > MOVING *ON* > > > > > > MOVING *ON*

Planning involves careful consideration of many aspects of the learning context. Identify the areas that you need to prioritise for your own development and consider how you will address them.

9
Assessment in RE

Chapter objectives

By the end of this chapter you will:

- **understand the role of assessment in RE;**
- **appreciate how assessment contributes to the learning process in RE;**
- **have considered the features of effective assessment in RE;**
- **be able to identify effective assessment strategies in RE;**
- **understand the role of recording and reporting in RE.**

This chapter addresses the following Standards for QTS: **Q11, Q12, Q26, Q27, Q28**

Introduction

Assessment is a dominant feature of the English education system. National targets and priorities draw our attention to how well children may be doing across the curriculum (Standard Q11). In this chapter we focus on the purpose of assessment in RE and the role it plays in promoting children's learning. We consider the limitations of what can be assessed and explore the best strategies for assessing different types of learning. We also discuss the value of using 'levels' of attainment in RE and the issues that need to be considered in relation to assessing, recording and reporting children's learning.

The place and value of assessment in RE

As we saw in Chapter 1, as far as RE is concerned, there are no national requirements, attainment targets or curriculum. Neither are there any national assessment requirements. Schools, therefore, must go to the syllabus they are required to use (either a local authority Agreed Syllabus or a religious foundation one), to see what it has to say about assessment.

All local authority syllabuses have a section on assessment and this is often informed by QCA guidelines, including the National Framework for RE (QCA, 2004). A good deal of this guidance is influenced by the assessment arrangements for the National Curriculum subjects, using the same language. In RE, therefore, it is possible to speak of 'Attainment Targets' and 'Levels of Achievement' even though these are not nationally prescribed.

The QCA National Guidelines describe eight levels of attainment for RE (QCA, 2004, pp34–7), with the expectation that most children at the end of the primary phase should reach level 4. The levels address the two QCA Attainment Targets: Learning about Religion and Learning from Religion (see Chapter 1). Teachers can use these, and their syllabus guidelines, to check on the progress their children are making in RE. (See below for guidance on using levels.)

As with any other subject, we need to be careful that we don't let assessment concerns dominate our thinking about what children learn in RE. There is a limit as to what we can assess in any subject, and we need to be sensitive to this probably more in RE than in other subject. It is easy to see how we can assess knowledge and understanding. We can find a variety of strategies to find out what children know and understand about a religious tradition, from informal question and answer sessions at the end of lessons, to formal examinations. We can also assess the skills that children are using by watching them work and examining their finished work. However there are some aspects of RE which are more difficult to assess, and even some which we should not attempt to assess.

An important part of RE relates to the attitudes towards others and their religions that children are developing. If these are important aspects of RE, we need to find ways of ascertaining what children's thinking is. How do we do this? Can we 'measure' how far children are sensitive to the perspectives of others, or have empathy with them? In the case study below the teacher demonstrates his commitment to fostering children's empathy with others.

CASE STUDY

The children in Amir's Year 5 class had been learning about Shabbat. They understood that Jewish families use Shabbat to focus on God and avoid doing work on that day. Amir introduces them to 'Michael', whose family is Jewish. Michael has a problem. It is Saturday morning and his family has just got back from synagogue. As they reach their home, two of Michael's friends see him and ask if he can join a football match they are having. Michael loves football. What thoughts might be going through his mind as his friends wait for their answer?

Amir asks the children to discuss Michael's problem. They then share their thoughts as a whole class.

In this assessment activity the children have to use their knowledge of Shabbat to understand why Michael has a problem. They need to know that his family are likely to avoid playing competitive sports on Shabbat and that although Michael loves football, his commitment to Shabbat will be foremost in his mind. The teacher, Amir, would be listening for discussion which demonstrates sensitivity to Michael's predicament. This would show not only an understanding of the Shabbat rules, but an awareness that living by those rules demands commitment and sacrifice.

We need also to recognise that RE is a very personal subject and that we must respect children's privacy. This means that we will not be assessing children's own religious commitments and beliefs. We will not be trying to discover how far religion influences their daily life, or whether they hold particular beliefs about God. And while we are hopeful that RE can contribute to children's spiritual and moral development, we will not be attempting to discover exactly where they are up to with these. To this end it is important that we offer children the opportunity not to respond to sensitive issues, if they feel uncomfortable with this. We must also protect younger children who may not be able to consent to sharing their thoughts, by avoiding asking them questions of a personal nature.

Assessment for learning

When we begin to think about assessment in RE, the first thing we need to consider is what it is for. Remember that there is no national requirement to report on children's achievements in RE, so our reasons for doing it must relate to our own practice and the development of the children we are teaching. The term 'assessment for learning' draws our attention to the purpose of assessment in RE. We do it because in some way it helps children to learn. How can assessment help children to learn in RE?

Assessment can:

- give us information on what children know and understand at a point in time;
- help us to identify misunderstandings that the children might have;
- allow us to plan for future development;
- allow us to plan for individual learning needs;
- help us to evaluate our own practice.

Assessment takes many different forms, the most common being 'formative' and 'summative'.

Formative assessment is usually thought of as identifying and celebrating what the child understands or can do and then identifying what the child needs to do next. Standard Q26 says that teachers need to *assess the learning needs of those they teach in order to set challenging learning objectives.* Formative assessment can be done at any point during the learning process to inform the next stage of learning. It is often used to plan the next lesson in a series of lessons. Activities that are helpful for formative assessment are ones that ask children to share what they know about a topic.

CASE STUDY

At the beginning of a new topic on 'Stories about Jesus' Joan asked her Year 2 class to think of any stories they remembered. She gave them a few minutes to talk to their friends and share any stories they knew. She then gave all the children a pile of sticky notes and asked them to draw a simple picture that gave a clue to the stories they could remember. To give them an idea of what she wanted, Joan took a note herself and quickly drew a coin. She told the children she knew of a story that Jesus told about a lady who lost a coin. The class spent the next 15 minutes drawing. The class came together to share their work, grouping similar pictures which they felt showed the same story. From this activity, Joan realised that while many of the children knew about the stories of Jesus' birth, only a few knew any more. She also identified four children who were familiar with several stories.

Summative assessment identifies what the child has learned at the end of a project, unit or period of time. It may be formal and it may be used to record progress so that it can be reported to parents or other interested parties. Summative assessment activities would include formal examinations, but can also be less formal. For example, the teacher might ask the children to write a final report at the end of a topic, design a display or write a booklet as information for someone else.

CASE STUDY

Stuart's Year 3 class had been learning about the life of a Muslim girl called Aysha. The end of the project coincided with their class's turn to lead the whole school assembly on a Friday. Stuart told the class that it was their turn for assembly and that he thought it would be a good idea for them to share their work about Aysha with the school.

He asked the class to think about what they felt they needed to tell the others about Aysha. The class worked in groups to gather their thoughts. They came up with the following list:

- Aysha goes to the mosque on Friday
- She doesn't eat pork
- She prays five times a day
- She likes to hear stories about Muhammad
- She wants to fast like her mum and dad but she is not allowed yet
- She thinks Eid is the happiest time
- She is learning to read Arabic
- She calls God 'Allah'

From this Stuart was able to identify the aspects of the topic that had stuck in the children's minds.

It is important that children are involved in the assessment process at every point. They need to know:

- why the teacher wants to assess their learning;
- what the teacher is going to assess;
- what the teacher will be looking for in any piece of work;
- what specific criteria the teacher will use for judging their work;
- how they can best meet the criteria and produce a good standard of work.

For example, if children are to write their own account of an event, they need to know the kind of thing that should be included so that they are clear about what the task demands.

PRACTICAL TASK PRACTICAL TASK PRACTICAL TASK PRACTICAL TASK PRACTICAL TASK

In the example below the teacher wants the children to demonstrate their understanding of Shabbat in Judaism by writing a diary entry. Her instructions to the Year 5 class are as follows.

Year 5 RE task Monday a.m.

Imagine you are a child from a Jewish family. You keep a diary of your life in and out of school. On Sunday you decide to write up how you spent Shabbat this week. What would you write?

Your writing should include:

– your learning from your study of Shabbat

– something about the how the family gets ready for Shabbat

– times of the day that are important

– the activities the family might do during Shabbat

– how the child feels during Shabbat

– why Shabbat is a special day for the child.

Consider the task that the children were set.

- How clear are the instructions?
- What knowledge is required?
- What skills are required?
- How does the teacher make the assessment criteria clear?
- Would you change or add to the instructions in any way?

It is common for teachers to display **learning objectives** for each lesson, so that the children understand what it is they should be learning. This is only useful if the objectives are presented in a way that is meaningful to them. It is equally important that the assessment criteria are presented in child-friendly language; for example, 'my work shows I can explain why Christian babies are baptised' is preferable to: 'the children will articulate the significance of baptism in Christianity'.

PRACTICAL TASK PRACTICAL TASK **PRACTICAL TASK** PRACTICAL TASK **PRACTICAL TASK**

Consider the following learning objectives. Re-write them as child-friendly assessment criteria. Use sentences starting 'I can...'

Foundation Stage

By the end of the activity the children will be able to articulate their feelings about the story of Rama and Sita

Key Stage 1

By the end of the activity the children will be able to communicate their understanding of 'new life in spring' through music

Key Stage 2

By the end of the activity the children will be able to reflect on sources of authority in their own lives

---

Assessment strategies

Assessment needs to be seen as an integral part of the planning and teaching cycle. The QTS Standards say that we must *know a range of approaches to assessment, including the importance of formative assessment* (Q12). As soon as we identify learning objectives, we can begin to identify what and how achievement might be assessed. In the box below, some learning objectives are listed. Next to them are the assessment criteria by which achievement might be identified. The last three are left blank for you to complete.

Lesson objectives By the end of the lesson the children will:	Assessment criteria Can the children:
be able to explain why the cross is a symbol of Christianity (Year 2)	explain why the cross is a symbol of Christianity?
be able to express their understanding of the term 'peace' (Year 4)	express their understanding of the term: 'peace'?
have extended their understanding of the festival of Diwali (Year 3)	describe the festival of Diwali in detail?
be able to re-tell the story of Jonah (EYFS)	
recognise the five symbols of membership to Sikhism (Year 5)	
talk about which questions they find puzzling and why (Year 1)	

The next stage is to identify how the learning is to be assessed. We need to recognise that assessment can take place during as well as after an activity. If we are assessing the skills children are developing, it might be that we need to observe them working. If we are assessing their knowledge, we might look at their completed work. The choice of activity we decide to plan will help us to identify the way in which we will assess. Let us take the three assessment criteria from the box shown on page 120:

> *Can the children:*
> - *explain why the cross is a symbol of Christianity? (Year 2)*
> - *express their understanding of the term 'peace'? (Year 4)*
> - *describe the festival of Diwali in detail? (Year 3)*

In the box below, the activity that will be used as the assessment is described and the teacher's notes relating to what she will be looking for are outlined.

Assessment criteria Can the children:	Assessment activity:	In the children's work I will be looking for:
explain why the cross is a symbol of Christianity? (Year 2)	The children will draw a picture of a cross and inside it write words they associate with it. Title of piece: 'When Christians look at the cross they think of...'	words such as Jesus, God, God's son, death, Easter, spring, crucifixion, resurrection, Good Friday, sadness, new life, heaven
express their understanding of the term 'peace'? (Year 4)	The children will create a group dance on the theme of 'peace'	Interpretation of the music, facial expression, type of movement, narrative, relationships, collaboration
describe the festival of Diwali in detail? (Year 3)	The children will design a leaflet called 'Celebrating Diwali'	Images and words associated with Diwali – lamps, Rama, Sita, Ravanna, Lakshmi, light. Descriptions of how Diwali is celebrated

It is clear that we cannot assess all lessons, all children, all the time. Practicalities make it important to select and target certain times, activities, children, subjects, areas of the classroom and so on. We may assess in a wide variety of ways, depending on the age of the children, the resources available, the type of activity and the reason why we are assessing.

Assessment through observation

Observation is a very useful assessment tool, used widely in the Early Years Foundation Stage, but less so further up the school. It is a valuable way of monitoring children's learning when they are:

- learning through play;
- learning through independent activity;
- taking part in discussion;
- involved in practical tasks;
- involved in collaborative tasks;
- using specific skills;
- experimenting;
- constructing.

Observation enables the teacher to see the processes children use, how they make decisions and choices, how they communicate with their peers and how they make use of resources. The teacher can gain a good sense of the child's learning strategies and observe where the child might have difficulty.

CASE STUDY

Sue's Year 6 class are discussing 'rules to live by'. In small groups they have to come up with a set of ten rules that they think would make the world a better place. Sue designs an observation schedule for herself which she can use to make notes as the children are working.

The schedule has three focal points:

1 What kind of contribution does the child make to the discussion?
2 What discussion skills does the child display?
3 Which rules does the child offer?

At the beginning of the task Sue tells the children that while they are working she will be moving from table to table listening to them talking. She tells them she will be listening for their contributions to the discussion. The children are used to Sue doing this and take little notice of her as she jots down brief notes as she visits their table. Sue knows that she will only capture a few minutes of each group's discussion, but over the year she hopes she will be able to get a good insight into the expressed views of the different children in her class.

Observation is a skilled and complex task, and we need to be realistic about how much we can observe at one time. One source of help for us is to use the other adults who may be working with us in the classroom. In many classrooms today there is more than one adult present – this could be a teaching assistant, a volunteer, a parent, a support worker or a trainee teacher. Each of these can support the teacher in their observations. For example, the teacher might be working with the whole class at the beginning or end of a lesson. In this situation it is very difficult for the teacher to observe or note the contributions of all the children. However, an assistant sitting nearby, but not part of the lesson, can easily make notes.

PRACTICAL TASK PRACTICAL TASK PRACTICAL TASK PRACTICAL TASK PRACTICAL TASK

Think of a time when you were working with a whole class at the beginning of a lesson. Perhaps you were introducing a new topic or reviewing a previous lesson. At some point you will have asked the class questions or asked for their contributions to assess what they know or understand already. How could another adult have helped you to identify:

- who contributed and who didn't?
- who appeared to have a good understanding and who didn't?
- who appeared engaged in the activity and who didn't?

Another way of assessing children as they work is to make use of ICT. Many teachers now use a tape recorder, digital camera or video recorder to record children's work. Some may get children to use the equipment to record their own and each other's work. The clear advantage of these methods is that they can be reviewed later and can give a picture of the event that notes may not be able to. They can also be offered as evidence for non-written work and shown to parents to show them how their child is working in school.

Assessment of work produced

When we think of assessment we often think of written work and marking. However, the product of children's work can vary and may include:

- written work;
- art work;
- design work;
- physical work;
- construction;
- musical composition;
- dance composition;
- dramatic composition.

For each of these types of work we need to be very clear what it is that we are expecting children to produce. We also need to be aware of the different expectations we might have of different children. For example, if the children are asked to do a piece of writing, say a report of an event, what exactly would the teacher be looking for in their writing? Although it is a writing task, our priority should not be, for example, the quality of the handwriting. It should instead be what the writing demonstrates about the child's understanding of religion. Similarly, if the children are to create a picture of a story they have heard, what details would the teacher expect to see? How would we evaluate a child's religious understanding as opposed to that child's artistic competence?

PRACTICAL TASK PRACTICAL TASK PRACTICAL TASK PRACTICAL TASK PRACTICAL TASK

Below are some descriptions of tasks given to children. What features might you be looking for in their work? The first one is done for you.

Task The children have:	Assessment criteria What would I be looking for?
Written a letter home from Makkah about their experience of Hajj	Details about different parts of Hajj – clothing, the Ka'aba, journey to Medina, throwing stones Feelings associated with Hajj – excitement, nervousness, closer to Allah
Used collage to convey their thoughts on 'creation'	
Designed a pattern for a prayer mat	
Created a dance expressing 'joy'	
Used blocks to build a church	
Composed a song to celebrate the Jewish festival of Hanukkah	
Performed a short scene about Jesus' arrest	

Self-assessment

Children should be able to recognise their own progress, so they need to know how to evaluate their own work (see Standard Q28). This needs to be part of the whole school's philosophy so that children become familiar with the approach and therefore more accurate in their assessment of themselves. It is a valuable skill for children to learn because it is one they can take into their future adult life, enabling them to be confident in expressing their own strengths and identifying what they need to do in order to progress further. It is a skill that enables them to be autonomous as learners and more likely to continue learning throughout their life.

How, then, do we begin to allow children to take a role in their own assessment? Like anything else that is new to children, it has to be introduced gradually and with lots of preparation and guidance. If they are introduced to the concept early in their education, it becomes just another part of what they do 'in school'. In many schools, self-assessment is introduced in the Early Years Foundation Stage, where children are invited to comment on the work they have done. Some schools use a 'smiley face' system in which children draw how they felt about doing the task. The teacher can then have a conversation with the children about why they chose that face to represent their feelings.

Higher up the school a similar system can be used, but here we would expect children to be able to articulate why they enjoyed a task or not, what they found easy or difficult, what they did or did not understand.

Children can summarise their own learning at the end of a topic by listing things they know and can do. See below the example of a Year 3 child's summary of learning after a topic on the role of the Qur'an in Islam.

> *Five things I have learned about the Qur'an*
> *1 It is a very special book*
> *2 Muslim people like to read it*
> *3 It is written in a language called Arabic*
> *4 It tells people how they should live*
> *5 They look after it very carefully*
>
> Gemma, age 8

Critical to any attempt to have children assess their own work is the teacher's role in:

- explaining the value of self-assessment;
- ensuring that the task is understood;
- ensuring that the criteria are understood;
- supporting children in their self-assessment;
- establishing a safe and secure atmosphere.

Each of these is needed in order that children understand the process and feel that their work and their view of it is valued. Children will need to be trained in how to assess their own work, how to recognise their own knowledge, understanding and skills as well as how to identify the gaps in their knowledge, understanding and skills. They will need help in setting development targets that are specific and achievable.

Some teachers are sceptical of children's ability to evaluate their own work critically.

Below are some comments that teachers who were new to children's self-assessment made. Discuss the comments with a colleague and suggest ways in which these problems might be overcome:

Concerns about self-assessment	Ways of addressing the concern
Children can't see where they have gone wrong	
Children will only focus on whether they have enjoyed the task or not	
Some children can be very self-critical if their self-esteem is low	
It could embarrass those who don't achieve so well	
They are unable to see how they could improve	

Peer assessment

A similar way of assessing children is using peer assessment. This is a process by which children use the criteria that have been established for evaluating a task, but instead of applying it to their own work, they use it to evaluate their colleagues' work. Such a strategy again needs careful introduction and implementation. The children need to be trained in peer assessment, which should include discussion of:

- the value of peer assessment;
- how to understand assessment criteria;
- how to give feedback;
- how to respond to peer feedback.

The children should be encouraged to come up with their own guidelines for effective peer assessment.

REFLECTIVE TASK

Consider the four discussion points above and answer the following questions.

- What is the value of peer assessment? Make a list.
- How can I make assessment criteria clear to all children?
- What are the features of effective, constructive feedback?
- How might we react to feedback?

Giving feedback

Children need to know how successful they have been in their learning and how they can improve their work, and this is where feedback is important (see Standard Q27).

Feedback can take place during and/or after an activity. Feedback during the activity helps to keep children focused, reassures them that they are on the right track and alerts them to any mistakes they might be making. Feedback after an activity tells the children how successfully they have completed a task, draws attention to particular strengths, alerts them to any misunderstandings and may identify improvements they might make to their work.

Feedback will usually be either verbal or written. Verbal feedback can take place during or after the activity and involves the teacher and child having a conversation about the work. The teacher might ask the child to describe or explain their work, or she might ask the child questions about their work. Written feedback is usually described as 'marking' and will often follow a set policy that is shared by the school.

Any feedback needs to take into account the child's previous achievement levels, individual learning needs and the child's feelings about the work. Confident learners are those who feel their work is valued and who believe they can succeed. It is the teacher's responsibility therefore to promote these feelings of confidence and success when giving feedback of any kind. Most feedback should, therefore, begin with a celebration of what the child has done well, before any criticisms of work are offered. Any criticism needs to be constructive, alerting the child to what is not satisfactory or could be developed and identifying why. The child should then be offered strategies or suggestions that would help them to improve their work. These are usually referred to as 'targets' which the child can then work on. It is important not to give children too many targets, nor must we feel that every piece of completed work has to have future targets allocated to it. Children should be able to have a feeling of completion and a job well done.

PRACTICAL TASK PRACTICAL TASK PRACTICAL TASK PRACTICAL TASK PRACTICAL TASK

Below are some examples of written feedback. Which ones are useful, recognising children's efforts, knowledge and skills and suggesting ways forward? Which ones are limited in their usefulness and why?

(a) Good work, Peter!

(b) You have described the festival very well, Hannah.

(c) A very accurate drawing of the Mosque, well done.

(d) You have explained pilgrimage very well. Can you give some examples of different pilgrimages you know of?

(e) Lovely pictures of you as a baby and now. How much you have grown!

(f) Great start to the diary, Jack.

(g) Have another look at the story. You have missed some out.

(i) This is not what you were asked to do.

Using levels to monitor learning

QCA guidance and local authority syllabuses suggest that we can monitor children's progress in RE using 'levels' of achievement. In the QCA National Framework, for example, level 1 describes the earliest level of children's understanding as they begin to learn about RE in school:

Level 1

Attainment Target 1 *Children use some religious words and phrases to recognise and name features of religious life and practice. They can recall religious stories and recognise symbols, and other verbal and visual forms of religious expression.*

Attainment Target 2 *Children talk about their own experiences and feelings, what they find interesting or puzzling and what is of value and concern to themselves and others.*

(QCA, 2004, p36)

By the time they reach age 11, it is expected that this knowledge and understanding and these skills and values have developed into the following for most children:

Level 4

Attainment Target 1 *Children use a developing religious vocabulary to describe and show understanding of sources, practices, beliefs, ideas, feelings and experiences. They make links between them, and describe some similarities and differences both within and between religions. They describe the impact of religion on people's lives. They suggest meanings for a range of forms of religious expression.*

Attainment Target 2 *Children raise, and suggest answers to, questions of identity, belonging, meaning, purpose, truth, values and commitments. They apply their ideas to their own and other people's lives. They describe what inspires and influences themselves and others.*

(QCA, 2004, p36)

The suggestion is that children's religious knowledge, understanding, skills and values are developmental and incremental and this draws our attention to the fact that we need to set suitable challenges for children if they are to deepen, widen and extend their understanding. (See Chapter 8 about progression and development.)

PRACTICAL TASK PRACTICAL TASK PRACTICAL TASK PRACTICAL TASK PRACTICAL TASK

- Examine the two level descriptions in the boxes above.
- Identify the different aspects of RE achievement that are described.
- Compare those of level 1 with those of level 4.
- What similarities are there?
- What differences are there?
- In what ways is it possible to see progression from level 1 to level 4?

The QCA guidance makes it clear that not all aspects of children's RE can be 'levelled' and that one piece of work is not enough to make an overall judgement on children's attainment. Instead, several pieces of work need to be used alongside other information, such as children's involvement in RE lessons and their responses to tasks given. Furthermore, a range of work may not fit exactly into one level or another, the best that can be achieved is matching a child's work to the level that best describes it.

PRACTICAL TASK PRACTICAL TASK PRACTICAL TASK PRACTICAL TASK PRACTICAL TASK

Below are examples of two children's RE work. The first is taken from notes made by the teacher as the child looked at a picture of Hanukkah at the end of a topic on that festival. The second is taken from a piece of writing which was done in response to 'Who was Muhammad?'. Which one would you say demonstrates a child working at QCA level 1, and which shows a child working at QCA level 4? Give reasons for your answers.

Sample 1

It's like Christmas, they get presents. They light candles every night. It's called Hanukah. They are Jewish, that's why the boys are wearing those hats. The light lasted for eight days in the temple. That's a game they play with counters. They are happy because they are having fun. I'm happy when it is Christmas.

Adam

Sample 2

Muslims believe he's the last prophet. He got the Qur'an from Allah and told other people about it. Muslims believe in Jesus too, but they don't believe he was God. They say Muhammad couldn't write so he had to get other people to write the Qur'an down. Muslim people behave the way the Qur'an tells them too. I do what my mum tells me to (and my teachers).

Ruth

Recording and using assessment data

Collecting assessment data is only useful if we put it to some use. The information we collect about children over a period of time can help us to support their learning in a variety of ways (see Standards Q26 and Q29).

Assessment data can be used for the following purposes:

- to plan future RE lessons;
- to monitor what RE learning has taken place;
- to pass on information about RE learning to other teachers;
- to report on RE to parents and others;
- to evaluate the effectiveness of our own teaching of RE;
- to evaluate the effectiveness of the school's provision for RE.

Assessment at the end of a lesson or series of lessons serves its purpose if it helps us to provide future learning activities which are well matched to the needs of the children. Written work is easy to record, and many teachers keep portfolios of children's work to monitor their progress. Evidence for progress in non-written work will need to be kept in the form of observation notes and/or photographs and film. Schools are obliged to give parents a report on how well their child is progressing in RE, even though no national attainment levels are required.

Often teachers will wish to pass on information about what the children have achieved in RE to the next teacher, as below.

CASE STUDY
Notes for Mrs Armstrong
Year 2 RE: Topics covered this year
  Who was Jesus?
  How do Christians celebrate Christmas?
  Caring for the World
  Stories from Islam
  Who Lives Around Here?
  The Church

The majority of the children are operating at around level 2. They are able to use religious language associated with the topics we have covered. They recognise that religion is important to many people. They know some Christian and Muslim stories and can explain why they are important to people. They are confident in expressing their own views about the world they live in and are aware of their responsibility to other people and their environment. They are able to explain why some behaviour is wrong.

Some children are operating more at level 1. They understand some religious terms and can remember parts of stories. They are less confident in expressing their views about religious matters.

One or two children are operating more at level 3. They are familiar with a number of religions and can identify features of them. They are aware that not all members of a religion believe the same thing. They can articulate the meaning behind some religious observances. They recognise where their own values come from.

When reporting RE progress to parents it is important to remember that they may not be familiar with particular religious terminology. It is expected that they will have some idea of what has been covered in RE across the year. Comments about children's progress should focus on their attitude to the subject and what knowledge and skills they have developed. It is also valuable to make particular mention of any very good pieces of work the child has produced.

CASE STUDY: EXCERPT FROM END OF YEAR 6 REPORT
Religious Education
  Matthew enjoys RE and takes part in discussion with enthusiasm. He likes to share his thoughts on puzzling questions and listens carefully to other people's views. He shows a good understanding of the topics we have covered and produced an excellent booklet on religious symbols.

Conclusion

Assessment is a valuable tool for helping you evaluate your teaching and address the needs of children. Try to get into the habit of incorporating it into your planning so that it becomes second nature to you in your planning for the subject.

A SUMMARY OF **KEY POINTS**

In this chapter we have explored:

> the value of assessment as an integral part of the learning process in RE;

> how assessment is used to promote children's learning in RE;

> the ways in which assessment can be incorporated into the main body of our work rather than added on at the end;

> the importance of being clear about the purpose of assessment, specific about the criteria and consistent in giving useful feedback;

> the value of involving the children at every stage of the assessment and planning cycle.

MOVING *ON* > > > **>** **>** **>** MOVING *ON* > > > **>** **>** **>** MOVING *ON*

Each local authority or diocesan syllabus will offer guidance for assessment in RE. Locate the syllabus for one of the schools you have worked in and read their guidance.

And moving on from this book:

This book has given you a start to teaching RE. You will find it useful to revisit it from time and to time to extend your own understanding by doing further reading. We hope that you will enjoy being a creative teacher in RE, one who is prepared to take risks, experiment, reviewing your practice for further development. We hope that you are already developing a real passion and interest in the subject which you will share with your children.

Appendix:
Introductions to six world religions

The introductions below give you a very brief overview of the major features of six world religions. They introduce you to the key terminology for each religion which you can use as the basis for further research as you prepare yourself to teach.

To further extend your subject knowledge we recommend that you start with the BBC website www.bbc.co.uk and follow links from there. Listening to relevant radio programmes such as *Beyond Belief* (Radio 4) and watching television programmes about religion will also help you become familiar with the material.

Suggestions for artefacts that can be bought and used in school are given at the end of each section.

Related Standards for QTS: **Q5, Q14, Q18**

1 Introduction to Buddhism

About six per cent of the world's population is Buddhist, the majority of whom live in the Indian sub-continent, China and South-east Asia. There are about 120,000 Buddhists in Britain, many of whom are Western converts. There is no belief in a transcendent God, but all forms of Buddhism recognise numerous 'supernatural' and god-like beings, although not everyone who calls themselves Buddhist would believe in their existence. Nor is there belief in a permanent unchanging soul; everything is changing and after death comes rebirth unless enlightenment has been achieved (see below).

The Buddha

Buddha means 'the Awakened'. A Buddha is not a god, but a human being who has awoken from the sleep of greed, hatred and confusion, in which it is believed all creatures usually live. Because he has developed perfect wisdom and compassion, he can help others to awaken. Buddhists believe that there may have been many such people. In particular, the title Buddha is given to the founder of Buddhism who lived in the 6th and 5th centuries BC.

Siddhattha Gotama (Siddhartha Gautama) was born near the border of Nepal with India in about 560 BC. According to tradition he was brought up in luxury as the son of the local ruler, protected from the world outside the palace. However, he begged his charioteer to take him beyond the walls. The sights of old age, sickness and death led him to be deeply troubled and he left home to become a wandering monk. He went to the most famous of religious teachers but none of them had the answer to human suffering. Then he tried extreme methods of self-deprivation but these turned out to be as useless as his former life of luxury. It is said that he then sat under a tree until he reached enlightenment. It was after this that he developed his own method of practice called the **Middle Way** because it avoids both extremes. He ate enough to live in a healthy way and discovered how to calm the mind by a form of meditation based on breathing.

The Buddha taught that a person who follows this path can experience the qualities of love, joy and compassion which are shared with all beings, and develop a mind that cannot be thrown off balance by pleasant or unpleasant things; a life free of selfish attachment will find release from this world of suffering – **Nibbana** (Nirvana). When the Buddha died, aged 80, he left his teaching, the **Dhamma**, as a guide, and the order of monks and nuns, the **Sangha**, to carry on his work.

Main spiritual leaders are believed to be the reincarnations of former leaders. The best-known Buddhist spiritual leader is the **Dalai Lama** of Tibet.

There are two main divisions in Buddhism – **Theravada** (mainly found in India, Sri Lanka and Thailand) and **Mahayana** (mainly found in China). Buddhism is sometimes wedded to local folk religions, for example, Chinese Buddhism is quite distinctive having within it aspects of Taoism, as well as local folk features. A key feature of Chinese Buddhism is belief that the forces of **Yin** (female) and **Yang** (male) must be kept in proper balance. Suffering and pain come when one is greater than the other. This balance also applies to the human body – illness is a result of imbalance of forces. Two of the main festivals of Chinese Buddhism are the **New Year Festival** in January/February and the **Moon Festival** in September.

Scriptures

The teaching is known as the **Dhamma**, ultimate reality. It is collected together in a series of texts written in **Pali** gathered over many years called the 'Pali canon'. It contains guidance for living, sayings and teachings said to have come from the Siddhartha himself, and the rules for the Buddhist community, the Sangha. It is customary for monks to learn sections of the scriptures by heart and then to recite them at festivals or other special occasions.

The Four Noble Truths

The major teachings of the Buddha, delivered in his first sermon, are called the Four Noble Truths.

The **First Noble Truth** maintains that all existence is suffering; the **Second** that the cause of suffering is desire, which fuels actions and leads to rebirth; the **Third** that the extinction of desire puts an end to suffering and leads to enlightenment and the escape from rebirth; the **Fourth** that the path to enlightenment is open to all people. This path is called the **Eightfold Path**.

The Eightfold Path

This is the path to enlightenment, and consists of:

(1) right knowledge, (2) right thought, (3) right speech, (4) right actions, (5) right livelihood, (6) right effort, (7) right mindfulness, (8) right concentration.

The principle of **kamma** (karma) is believed to affect everyone's lives. Whatever an individual thinks or does brings consequences, whether in this life or the next after reincarnation. Thus misfortune in the present life is often attributed to misdeed in the former. However, as one perfects Buddhist practice and teachings, turning from desire and the sense of self, the effects of kamma dissipate.

The Sangha was established by the Buddha. It is a community of monks and nuns who keep alive the knowledge the teachings of the Buddha (the Dharma) and live as closely as possible to the Buddha's teachings. Monks and nuns rely on gifts from the lay community for their food and clothing. In many countries they also provide medical care. People come to the monasteries to meditate, listen to the teachings or ask advice.

Buddhist devotion

Buddhists prefer the word devotion to worship. Buddhist devotional acts (**pujas**) take place in both home and temple, and while they may be occasions for being with others, they are essentially individual rather than communal acts. Puja is often offered in the morning and evening, and particularly at full and half moon. Artefacts and images are the focus for devotion to the Buddha; there is often a small shrine in the home containing an image of the Buddha. Sweet incense is often used. Buddhist homes are often festooned outside with prayer flags, and prayer wheels are also used.

Daily life

Buddhists try to follow the Eightfold Path in their daily lives. Many Buddhist homes have statues of the Buddha which may be a focus for daily meditation. Piety is expressed in giving to monks and nuns. There are no rules on dress or food though many Buddhists are vegetarian. Monks and nuns wear saffron coloured robes and shave their heads.

Initiation into the Sangha is marked by a special ceremony or **Ordination**. Becoming a monk or nun is not necessarily a life-long commitment, for example, in Thailand and Burma many boys enter the Sangha for a period between the ages of ten and 20. **Marriage** is not regarded as 'sacred' but a contracted partnership (divorce is acceptable). Simple vows are sometimes taken and monks and nuns may be present but are not required. Chastity is also highly valued as a way of life, because of the importance of the Sangha. A 'good' **death** is important and it is the duty of the relatives to help the dying person obtain it so that he or she may have the best possible rebirth within the restrictions of kamma (karma). Bodies are usually cremated.

Festivals

Wesak (Visakha) is usually in May or June. The major events of the Buddha's life – his birth, enlightenment and death – all happened on the same day in different years. Wesak celebrates his life and teaching. It is marked by acts of worship and decorating homes and temples with flowers and lanterns. Extra hospitality is given to the monks.

Dhammacakka, is celebrated around July, and commemorates the Buddha-to-be's conception and leaving home. It recalls the Buddha's first sermon after gaining enlightenment. It also marks the beginning of the 'Rains', the three months when Buddhist monks should remain in one residence and which is traditionally a time of increased contact between monks and laity. People visit monks to take them gifts of food and to hear them preach and read the scripture.

Places of pilgrimage

Places associated with the Buddha's life:

Lumbini Grove in Nepal: the place of his birth;
Bodhi Tree in Bodhgaya, India: the place of his enlightenment;
Deer Park in Sarnath, India: the place of his first discourse;
Sala Grove in Kusinara, India: the place of his passing away.

Artefacts

Image of the Buddha, prayer wheel, Tanka (image on a silk cloth) and prayer flags.

2 Introduction to Christianity

Christianity began two thousand years ago in Palestine at a time of Roman rule among the followers of the itinerant Jewish preacher Jesus of Nazareth. The small first group has multiplied into a multicultural religion with over two billion followers. Those followers share some key beliefs and rituals but the ways in which those beliefs and rituals are interpreted and manifested are very varied, the differences being the consequences of ancient disputes and local factors. The Christian community in Britain (72% of the population) comprises people from Africa and Europe, especially Poland, as well as the older communities. The Western calendar is counted from the year of his birth.

Jesus

A belief that Jesus is the **Messiah**, the anointed one of God, is at the core of Christian belief. Jesus began a ministry at about the age of 30. He was known for his healing miracles, his teaching in sayings and short stories (**parables**) and for mixing with the poor and outcast. He preached repentance and that the love of God was expressed in the love of enemy and stranger. He was crucified by the Roman authorities at about the age of 33. His followers believe that he rose again from the dead after three days. The **Gospels** are four different accounts of his ministry and the events leading up to his death. These were probably written between 30 and 70 years after his death.

God (The Trinity)

Christianity teaches monotheism – one God with three ways of being: God the Father, God the Son and God the Holy Spirit. The Father indicates God's transcendence, the Son expresses God's presence in Jesus and in the suffering of the world, and the Holy Spirit expresses God active in the world.

Scriptures

The first Christians believed they were the true Jews and so the sacred books of the Jews became the old covenant or **Old Testament** of the Christian **Bible**. Later other texts were added to form the **New Testament**. These included the Gospels, and letters written by church leaders, mainly the apostle Paul, within the first decades after the death of Jesus. Some Christians have a literal belief in the Bible, including places where it runs counter to scientific accounts. Others reject literalist readings and see its truth lying in the power of narrative, poetry and in its witness to belief.

The church

The people of God are the church but is a divided one, broken into major traditions and factions – the Orthodox, the Roman Catholic and the Protestant tradition – but all are Christians. The differences are reflected in the church buildings and styles of worship. Worship in some, especially those with African links, often pulsate with vibrant energy, others are noted for the centrality of teaching from the scriptures, others are places of quiet reflection and tradition. For some the use of imagery is a valued means of focusing on the divine, gaining a glimpse of heaven, others reject the use of all visual imagery in worship.

Some churches have ministers – teachers and pastoral leaders. For others it is important that their leaders have an authority going back to the early church. Here the leaders are usually called **priests** because there are some rituals only they can perform, e.g. consecrating the bread and wine at the service of Holy Communion or **Eucharist**. Some churches emphasise equality in leadership, others have a hierarchy with bishops and archbishops.

Christianity came to Britain with the Romans. The state church in England is the Church of England, a protestant church which may be Catholic in style.

The sharing of bread and wine, begun by the early Christians in recall of the last meal Jesus had with his disciples, is central to much Christian worship. Protestant Christians believe it is an act of remembrance, Catholic Christians see it as a sacrament in which God is made present in the bread and wine.

Rites of passage

Baptism
Baptism dates back to the first Christians. The majority of Christians baptise babies and children as well as adults – seeing baptism as an act of grace by which the child enters the church. They then have their faith **confirmed** when they are teenagers. Others reserve baptism for adults – an outward sign of their conversion. Baptism can be a simple washing with water, or a plunging fully immersed into the water.

Marriage
Life-long monogamy is the ideal for Christians. The Roman Catholic Church does not recognise divorce.

Death
Christianity teaches that there is life after death; that all will be resurrected to a day of judgement. Some Christians have a literal belief in hell for those who don't follow Jesus; others are more agnostic and inclusive in their beliefs, having faith in a loving God.

Daily life

Prayer and Bible reading is a part of daily life. Loving one's neighbour as oneself is the guiding principle. Blessings may be said over food.

Festivals

The birth of Jesus is celebrated at the mid-winter festival of **Christmas** with its themes of light and hope and gift-giving. **Advent** prepares for Christmas. The triumph of good over evil, of life over death, is celebrated at the spring festival of **Easter** in the remembrance of Jesus' death and resurrection. **Lent**, a traditional time of abstinence, prepares for Easter. The coming of the Holy Spirit is celebrated 40 days after Easter at **Pentecost**.

Main places of pilgrimage

Jerusalem, Bethlehem and, for Roman Catholics, Rome.

Artefacts

Crucifix, painted cross, rosary beads used for prayer, Bible, icons, nativity crib scene.

3 Introduction to Hinduism

The term 'Hinduism' can give a misleading impression of an organised, homogeneous body of believers. In fact Hindus vary considerably both in belief and practice, and their faith has no founder. 'Hindus' was the name given to the inhabitants of the area of India round the river Indus.

It is estimated that there are about 950 million Hindus world-wide, with about 500,000 in Britain.

One important characteristic of Hinduism is its acceptance and inclusion of many varying beliefs and ways of worship, thus allowing for enormous variety, and making it impossible to give a full or indeed any single account of practices and beliefs.

Gods and goddesses

The **Vedas** (one Hindu scripture) teach one central Godhead, who is essentially unknowable, and has many manifestations. Everything in the universe embodies something of God for God is immanent in creation rather than separate. However, sometimes Hindus speak of a central trinity of gods: **Brahma** the creator, **Vishnu** the sustainer of the created order, and **Shiva** the destroyer.

There are many other manifestations of God, male and female. These include Vishnu's wife, **Lakshmi**, the goddess of wealth; the elephant-headed god **Ganesh**, patron of learning, good beginnings and the remover of obstacles. In addition, it is believed that the god Vishnu has manifested himself on earth in animal and human form in order to fight evil and restore the balance between good and evil. These manifestations are called **avatars**. Two of the avatars in human form are **Rama**, the perfect man, and **Krishna**, who is worshipped with particular devotion.

For some Hindus the gods have a separate literal existence. For others, the gods are symbols representing aspects of the universe.

Scriptures

The principal scriptures in Hindusim include the Vedas, written in the ancient language Sanskrit (reputedly around 1200 BCE), the **Upanishads,** (reputedly written about 800 BCE), the **Ramayana** (dating from about the 9th century BCE) and the **Mahabharata** (from the 6th century BCE).

The Ramayana tells the story of Rama and his wife, **Sita,** who are regarded as the perfect models of manhood and womanhood. The Mahabharata tells the story of the wars between two families of cousins, the Pandavas and Kauravas, over a disputed section of land.

Worship

The variety of the Hindu faith is reflected in the ways of worshipping. The aim of worship is to realise the oneness of the individual with the divine. There are several paths for this, all of equal merit including the paths of:

- knowledge through understanding the relationship between **atman** (the soul) and Brahma (the godhead);
- yoga or discipline, and right action according to one's **dharma** (one's duty according to position in life);
- **bhakti**, loving devotion to one's particular deity.

These paths can be combined but the specific emphasis is left to the individual.

Religious observance is largely home-based, and most Hindu homes will have a **shrine** to honour their own particular choice of deities. In a devout Hindu home, worship (**puja**) is made three times a day, morning, noon and night – and the form this takes may vary but usually involves lighting the **arti** lamp, a sacred flame using ghee or oil, and incense.

Attendance at a temple is not regarded as being a necessary part of a Hindu's religious duties, but rather one of many ways of helping the individual to grow closer to God. In the UK temples serve as both social and religious focal points for the Hindu community. Services are often held every evening, but many people will attend on Sunday, when the main service of the week takes place in Britain. Priests of the Brahmin caste perform rituals in the temples and in people's homes. The arti fire, having been offered to the deities, is then passed amongst the worshippers. The blessings of the deities are shared by passing one's hands over the flame and then over the face and head.

Daily life

The caste system

The caste system originated as a way of clarifying the rights and duties of people in different walks of life. The four main divisions of caste are: **Brahmins**, priestly class; **Kshatriyas**, soldiers; **Vaishyas**, farmers and merchants; **Shudras**, manual labourers. In addition there are the Untouchables or **Harijans.** (This name, meaning Children of God, was given by Gandhi in his efforts to improve their lot.) These do work that is polluting, such as leather work, involving the dead bodies of animals. The system has come under criticism because of its rigidity, and in some areas is now relaxing somewhat, particularly in Britain.

Food

There are no particular rules for Hindus, but because of the principle of **ahimsa**, non-violence, many Hindus are vegetarians. Beef is not eaten as cows are sacred though milk products are taken freely. Before eating, a small portion of food is offered before the shrine for a blessing from the god. This is then mixed with the rest of the food so that all the food is blessed.

Rites of passage

Many aspects of Hindu life, and particularly the ceremonies relating to birth and death, are shaped by the Hindu belief in reincarnation. The individual soul is destined to be reborn many times, in different bodies, whether human or animal, the circumstances of each rebirth being affected by the deeds in previous lives, **karma**. The aim is to live life as well as possible in accordance with the situation one is placed in, so that the next rebirth will be a better one.

A Hindu's life is divided into four distinct stages. The first begins with the initiation ceremony and marks the student stage. The second is the stage of the married householder. The third stage comes when a man has fulfilled his religious and social duties to his family. He hands over his duties to his household and spends his time reading holy books or he may devote himself to a cause, e.g. building a new temple.

The religious care of a **baby** and his preparation for a good life begin in the mother's womb, as the pregnant woman reads the scriptures to her baby. Several ceremonies mark different stages of the baby's life. Boys of the three upper castes at the age of seven or older may take part in the **sacred thread ceremony**. At this ceremony the boy is given a thread of three strands which he must always wear. Vows are taken accepting the duties of being a man.

A Hindu **marriage** is an alliance of two families, and it is often the case that the married sons continue to live in their father's house. Parents usually choose a marriage partner for their child, usually from the same caste. A Hindu wedding is a very long and elaborate ceremony, at which different relatives of the bride and groom have specific roles to play.

The Hindu treatment of **death** is closely bound up with the belief in reincarnation. The body is always cremated, which should be done as soon as possible after death. In India this is done on a funeral pyre of wood, in Britain at a crematorium.

Festivals

In India there is great variation in what festivals are celebrated and how, depending on local tradition and which gods are particularly worshipped. However, some festivals are universally celebrated, and it is mainly these that are celebrated in this country. They include the following.

- **Holi**, in March–April. This festival combines elements of a spring festival with celebration of the pranks that Krishna played as a young man. Also involved is a story about a demon goddess called **Holika**. It is celebrated with bonfires and by squirting coloured water at each other, and general tricks and good fun.
- **Rama Naumi**, in March–April, celebrating the birthday of Rama. A model of baby Rama in a cradle is set up in the temple.
- **Raksha Bandhan**, in August. The main ceremony is tying a silk thread, with a flower, to the wrists of others. In some places this is done for friends and relatives by the head of the household, others celebrate the day as sisters' day, and sisters tie the threads on their brothers' wrists.

- **Janmashtami**, in August–September. This festival celebrates the birth of Krishna and his miraculous delivery from the demon **Kansa** who wished to kill him. A feature of the worship at this festival is a picture or statue of the child Krishna on a swing, which people take turns to push, to keep him amused.
- **Dusshera** (**Durga puja**, or **Navaratri**) in September or October. This celebrates the most important female deity, **Devi** (consort of Shiva), who has many forms and about whom many stories are told. As **Kali** she destroys time, as **Parvati** she is the faithful wife of Shiva, as **Durga** she is the destroyer of evil demons. The festival lasts ten days, during which time different manifestations of the goddess are honoured, and stories told.
- **Diwali**, in October, is the most widely celebrated Hindu festival. It is celebrated in many different ways, and combines many elements – the most important of which is the New Year, when traders close their old accounts and open new account books and pray to Lakshmi, goddess of wealth. At this time also is the celebration of the return from exile of Rama and Sita, symbolising the triumph of good over evil. Arti lamps are lit in every window, and paper effigies of the demon Ravana are burnt.

Holy places

Throughout India there are places which are particularly associated with certain deities, and others which are more generally holy. The river **Ganges** is holy throughout its length, and particularly so in certain places such as **Varanasi**. Pilgrimage to holy places is recognised as being one means for the individual to grow closer to God, but there is no duty of pilgrimage. It is undertaken only if the individual feels it will help them in their religious quest.

Artefacts

Small statues of the gods, puja tray.

4 Introduction to Islam

The word Islam means submission to the will of God in all things. Three per cent of the British population is Muslim. Muslims live throughout the world, with the biggest populations being in the Middle east, the Indian sub-continent and Indonesia. The world-wide community of Islam is called the **Umma**.

The two main divisions in Islam are **Sunni** (the larger) and **Shi'a**. **Sufi'ism** is the mystical tradition within Islam.

The Prophet Muhammad

All Muslims accept that Muhammad was the final prophet. 'Peace be Upon Him' is often said after his name as a mark of the respect. Muhammad was a trader in Arabia in the 7th century CE. Muslims believe that the angel Jibra'eel (Gabriel) appeared to him in a cave at Hira outside the city of Mecca where he lived, and instructed him to memorise words which called people to worship one true God. This message of monotheism clashed with the polytheistic practices and he was initially persecuted. He and his followers left Mecca (the **Hijrah**) in 622 CE, the first year of the Muslim calendar. A period of missionary, political and military activity followed so that by the time of the Prophet's death in 632 CE Islam was established in most of the Arabian peninsular, including Mecca itself.

The Qur'an

The **Qur'an** is the collection of all the revelations Muslims believe were given to Muhammad by the angel. As the words are regarded as the direct transmission from God himself, the Qur'an is read and studied in the original Arabic and translations are never used in worship. The book contains teachings about God, daily life and disputes and refers to Jesus and figures in ancient Judaism. It does not contain stories about the life of Muhammad. Muslims consider the Qur'an to be the foundation of all other knowledge. Islam teaches that the Qur'an is the final revelation, superseding the Jewish Torah and the Christian Bible.

Reading of the Qur'an is an important part of Muslim faith. Passages from the Qur'an are also used to adorn buildings and artefacts.

Copies of the Qur'an are always treated with great care. They are wrapped in clean cloths and kept on a high shelf and placed on a bookrest for reading. Ritual washing occurs before handling the text. The book is not venerated as a physical object but is respected as the word of God.

Children often attend after-school classes in the local mosque so that they can learn to read Arabic and recite the Qur'an. A Muslim schoolchild will often be learning three languages, the mother tongue of the home, e.g. Urdu, English and Arabic.

The laws of Islam (**Shar'ia**) is based on the Qur'an in a strict traditional code of interpretation. This includes looking to the **Hadith**, stories of the life of the Prophet, whose life exemplifies the living of the Qur'an.

The Five Pillars of Faith

1 **The declaration of faith.** 'There is no God but God and Muhammad is his prophet.' Islam is a strictly monotheistic religion. The Qur'an forbids the worship of idols; no images are made of God or the Prophet. Many Muslims today object to any pictures of humans. Allah strictly translates as God. In the Qur'an Allah is spoken of with 99 names, each one saying something of his character (e.g. Revealer, Sustainer, Judge, the All-wise, the All-Compassionate). Muslims often think about God by reciting these names with the help of **prayer beads**.
2 **Prayer – Salah.** Five daily prayer times are laid down at specified intervals round the length of the day. Prayers should be preceded by **wudu**, ritual washing, in a specified order. These prayers are set, undertaken facing Mecca, and involve different postures including kneeling. A clean surface is needed, usually a prayer mat. On Fridays Muslim men are expected to perform the after-midday prayer in the mosque. Women sit upstairs or pray at home. At the end of set prayers, the worshipper adds his or her own prayers silently, maybe asking God for forgiveness, for guidance or giving thanks for particular blessings. After communal prayers handshakes are exchanged.
3 **Fasting (sawm).** The ninth Muslim month, **Ramadan**, is a month of fasting: adult Muslims do not allow any food or liquid to enter the mouth from sunrise to sunset. It is a time to learn discipline and identify with the poor. Women menstruating, travellers and the sick are also exempt but must make up the time later. Since the Islamic calendar is lunar, Ramadan occurs gradually earlier each Western year.
4 **Welfare tax (zakat).** An annual 2.5 per cent tax on surplus wealth is made to help the poor.

5 **Pilgrimage (Hajj).** Muslims try to perform the pilgrimage to Mecca during the month of pilgrimage at least once in a lifetime. All wear a simple white garment as a mark of equality with others and humility before God. There are many rituals to perform during the pilgrimage including the circumlocution of the **Ka'aba**, a sacred cuboid black building.

The mosque

A mosque is a place set aside for private and communal prayer. The **mihrab**, a niche in the wall, marks the direction of Mecca. A small set of steps, a **minbar**, is used by the **imam**, the teacher and pastoral leader, for the Friday sermon. A series of clock faces show the prayer times for that day. Chairs are absent except perhaps a few along walls for the disabled. There is a separate section for women. The mosque may be decorated with abstract patterns, words from the Qur'an and sometimes pictures of the Ka'aba. Outside the main room of the mosque are facilities for ritual washing (wudu), and often also a school and meeting rooms. There is usually a place to prepare the dead for burial.

Daily life

Many details of daily life are laid down in the Qur'an or the Hadith.

Food
Any meat eaten must be slaughtered in the correct way, including invoking the name of God. This is called **halal** meat. Alcohol and pig meat are forbidden. 'Bismallah', 'In the name of God', is said before eating.

Dress
Men and women are required to dress modestly, covering the whole body with loose clothing, but style may vary according to local culture. For women this means covering the whole body in public, except for the face and hands. Many Muslim women now wear the headscarf, the **hijab**, and some cover their faces (**niqab**).

Rites of passage

Birth
The call to prayer is whispered into a baby's ear as soon as possible after birth. Other customs vary according to the country of origin. All boys must be circumcised, but not necessarily at birth.

Marriage
Arranged marriages are common but the Qur'an decrees that the girl must give her consent and not be forced to marry. Marriage is essentially a contract between the two people. Divorce is permitted but vigorously discouraged.

Death
After death the body is ritually washed and wrapped in a white shroud, and should be buried as soon as possible. Prayers are said by the community, affirming the power over life and death. Excessive grief is discouraged as it is assumed that someone who dies as an observant Muslim will go to Paradise. There is a belief in a final judgement day.

Festivals

There are two main festivals in Islam:

- **Eid ul-Fitr.** This celebrates the end of the month of fasting. It is heralded by the sight of the new moon. Themes are obedience and self-discipline.
- **Eid ul-Adha.** This celebrates the willingness of the prophet Ibrahim (Abraham) to sacrifice his son Ishmael when God asked it of him. A lamb was sacrificed instead of Ishmael on God's command, so the sacrifice of a lamb or goat is an important part of the festival. There is also the culmination of the Hajj.

Places of pilgrimage

Makkah (Mecca) is the holiest place in Islam and is now visited every year by about 3,000 million Muslims performing the Fifth Pillar of the faith. It is also the direction (Qibla) all Muslims face when they pray no matter where they are. **Medina**, situated north of Mecca, is where Muhammad is buried. The third holiest place is the **Dome of the Rock** in Jerusalem, where Muhammad is believed to have ascended to heaven.

Artefacts

Prayer beads, prayer mat, compass, head covering, Qur'an.

5 Introduction to Judaism

Judaism is both a religion and a cultural identity. A person is a Jew if they have a Jewish mother unless they have converted to another religion. The majority of Jews in Britain are **Orthodox**, although there are also many who belong to **Conservative**, **Liberal** and **Reform Judaism**. At present there are an estimated 330,000 practising Jews in Britain.

Judaism has its origins in the Hebrews or Israelites of the Ancient Middle East. The Jews were expelled from Jerusalem by Romans occupiers in the first two centuries CE after insurrections during which the great temple was destroyed. Israel became a Jewish state in 1948.

Scriptures and other religious writings

The term **Tenakh (Hebrew Bible)** refers to the whole of Jewish scripture and includes the Torah (the Law), the Psalms, the Prophets and the Writings.

The Torah

The **Torah** comprises the five books believed to be written by **Moses**. It contains the laws which govern Jewish life and the stories of the ancestors beginning with Adam and Eve and including Noah, Abraham and Moses. Each **synagogue** has at least one copy of the Torah, hand copied in the original Hebrew on a parchment scroll by a trained scribe. The scroll is protected by an embellished cover and kept in an **Ark**, a decorated cupboard. The Torah is read at the weekly Sabbath services and carried in procession during Simhat Torah.

Mishnah and Talmud

All Jewish life and practice is based on the Torah which is reinterpreted by the teachers, **rabbis,** for each generation in the light of the interpretations in the past. These interpretations are largely an oral tradition. Two major written collections of oral interpretations of the Torah, the Mishnah (2nd century BCE) and Talmud (6th century CE) are part of that tradition.

The synagogue and worship

The synagogue is the communal centre for prayer and study of the Torah often led by a **rabbi**. Ten Jewish men are required for a service (**minyan**). Preaching takes place from a raised platform, the **Bimah**. An eternal flame and the first line of each of the ten commandments are above the Ark.

In Orthodox and traditional synagogues men and women sit separately. In most Reform synagogues men and women may sit together. Synagogues may be decorated but have no images of people or animals as the law forbids the making of images.

Jewish men are required to say daily prayers at home. They usually wrap themselves in a prayer shawl, and during weekday prayers tie leather boxes (**tefillin**) containing the words of the **Shema** to their head, arm and hand, signifying keeping God's law in all they think, feel and do.

Beliefs

At the heart of Jewish belief is the Shema, found in **Deuteronomy 6: 4–7**. This begins: *Hear, O Israel: the Lord our God, the Lord is One.* God is creator, and Lord of all the universe with a special relationship with the Jewish people who have a vocation to be His people and keep His commandments. Images of God are forbidden and many Jews will not write the word, putting G–d instead.

Daily life

Jewish daily life follows the laws found in the Torah as interpreted by the rabbis. Much of the practice of the faith takes place in the home. Small boxes (**mezuzah**) containing the words of the Shema are placed on the right hand doorpost, reminding Jews to remember God in all comings and goings.

Jewish food laws (called **kashrut**) relate to what is eaten, how it is slaughtered, how prepared and cooked, and how eaten. Milk and meat must not be eaten in the same meal. Pork and most sea food is forbidden.

Yarmulka/kappa is a small cap worn by observant Jewish men to show that they are below God. Very Orthodox Jewish women wear wigs to cover their hair.

Rites of passage

Birth
Baby boys are circumcised by a trained **mohel**, on the eighth day after birth. Blessings take place for girls in the synagogue.

Bar mitzvah
When a Jewish boy is 13 years old he is regarded as being old enough to take responsibility for himself and his observance of the Law. He is in religious terms an adult, a 'son of the

commandment', **bar mitzvah** in Hebrew. In Progressive Jewish congregations girls, too, celebrate their coming of age at 12 years with a **bat mitzvah** (daughter of the command-ment) ceremony. Orthodox Jews have a **bat hayil** service for girls aged 12 on a Sunday afternoon.

Marriage

A Jewish wedding takes place (often on a Sunday, since it cannot be held on the Sabbath or festivals) under a canopy, the **hupah**, which is decorated with flowers and symbolises the new home the bride and groom will make together.

Death

Jews believe in the resurrection of the dead. The body must be buried as soon as possible after death, and is washed, anointed with spices and wrapped in a white sheet. Burial must be in Jewish consecrated ground. Mourning times and observations are formalised across the next 11 months for the family.

Festivals and holy days

The festivals fall in approximately the same Western month each year but the date varies. The new day begins at nightfall so festivals begin in the evening. The years are dated from the traditional Jewish dating of the creation of the world (about 5,600 years ago). The festivals are:

- The weekly festival **Shabbat** (day of rest). The observance of Shabbat (Sabbath) is laid down in the Torah. It begins with the lighting of candles and the Sabbath meal on Friday evening. During the Sabbath no work is done, no money is carried or business transacted. This is in celebration of the account of Creation in the Bible, where God rests on the seventh day. Everything is done to make the day special – best clothes, the best food that the family can afford, and families spend time together. Themes are family and creation.
- **Rosh Hashanah** and **Yom Kippur**: September. The Jewish New Year. Yom Kippur is the **Day of Atonement**, a day of complete fasting. Themes are repentance and forgiveness.
- **Sukkot**: September–October. Families have their meals and often sleep in temporary shelters built outside. This remembers the ancestors living in the desert.
- **Simhat Torah**: September–October, two days after Sukkot. This festival celebrates God's mercy in giving the Torah, and marks the end of the annual reading of the whole Torah.
- **Pesach or Passover**: March–April. The story of the escape from Egypt is remembered with family and community meals, readings from the **Haggadah** and lots of singing. The house is cleaned of all leavened products, including spirits. Bread must be unleavened (**matzos**). Symbolic food is placed on a **seder plate** and incorporated into the meal, which celebrates freedom from slavery.
- **Shavuot**: May–June. Commemorates the giving of the Law (Torah) to Moses on Mount Sinai.
- **Hanukkah**: December. A minor festival of lights which remembers the conquest of the Maccabees. Popular in Europe because it is mid-winter.
- **Purim**: February–March. A celebration of faithfulness; the story of Esther, the Jewish queen of the Persian king Xerxes, who saved her people from destruction by the king's minister Haman.

Places of pilgrimage

The remaining wall of the second Temple (the Western Wall) is a place of pilgrimage and prayer. Jerusalem is a holy city, Israel a holy country.

Artefacts

Prayer shawl, facsimile of the Torah, mezuzah.

6 Introduction to Sikhism

The Sikh religion began in the Punjab region of North-West India with the teachings of Guru Nanak, born 1469. There are 16 million Sikhs world-wide but most are still in the Punjab.

The Sikh gurus

In the Sikh religion a **'guru'** denotes one who leads one to the light/truth. God himself is the true Guru. The title Guru is also given to the ten successive spiritual leaders of the Sikh community.

Guru Nanak was born into a Hindu home in North-West India, at a time of tension between Hindu and Muslim. The many stories about his life tell of his wisdom, his devotion to truth, honesty, concern for the poor, and rejection of empty ritual. Above all he taught that the light of God is in everyone and all are equal. He was opposed to the caste system. He spent much of his life as an itinerant preacher until, in the final stage, he established a Sikh community, in which labour was not divided according to caste or status, and all ate together as equals.

At the end of his life he appointed as successor a man noted for his deep humility. This practice of each Guru naming his successor continued for approximately 200 years, until the tenth Guru, Guru **Gobind Singh**, decided against naming a single human successor. Instead he announced that the Sikh sacred book, the Guru Granth Sahib, would be the guide to the Sikh community, called the **Panth**, which would now make decisions in the presence of the holy book. Meanwhile the Sikh movement had become increasingly militaristic, with defence of religious freedom for all being a cause for which many Sikhs (including two of the Gurus) were martyred. There was also a great concern for social justice.

Sikhs believe that God has never taken human form so although highly respected, the Gurus are not worshipped.

The Sikh Holy Book – the Guru Granth Sahib

Granth means book, and Sahib is a title of respect, so Guru Granth Sahib means something like 'the highly respected book, God's messenger'. It is a collection of nearly 6000 hymns by the Gurus, with some by Hindus and Muslims. It is written in Gurmurki, the written language of the Punjab. Sikh children often attend classes in the language.

The Guru Granth Sahib is not worshipped but is treated with great respect. It rests on a bed of cushions with a canopy over it. When it is moved, it must be accompanied by five members of the **Khalsa** (see below). It has its own room in homes and is taken ceremonially to a separate room at night in the Sikh place of worship, the **Gurdwara** literally the 'home of the Guru'. The original copy of the Guru Granth Sahib is kept in the **Golden Temple in Amritsar** in the Punjab, a place of pilgrimage for Sikhs since the fifth Guru. During the service one member of the congregation sits behind the Guru Granth Sahib and at intervals waves the **chauri** (a type of whisk) over it, recalling the personal care of a living Guru in a hot country.

The Guru Granth Sahib is at the centre of all worship of God and Sikh life. Its hymns are part of the daily prayer of a Sikh. A key verse, the **Mool Mantra**, is whispered into a baby's ear at birth and the baby's name is chosen from the first letter of a random reading on the naming day. The bride and groom walk round the Guru Granth Sahib during **wedding ceremonies**, and it is read at **death**. It is read or sung by teams of readers in its entirety at festivals, a process taking three days.

Men and women share in the reading from Guru Granth Sahib during communal services in the Gurdwara. It is often sung to the accompaniment of the harmonium. The **Granthi**, the spiritual leader, may give an interpretation.

Services are usually held for convenience on a Sunday in Britain. As well as the sermon and reading, offerings are made and a sweet food, **kara prashad** is shared. People sit on the floor, men and women separately, and come and go.

Afterwards the community eats together a meal prepared by men and women in the **langar**, the free kitchen. This food is vegetarian so that those of other religions can join in, and all are equal. Families take it in turns to pay for and prepare the food. Sometimes this is in honour of a celebration such as a wedding anniversary.

The Khalsa

In 1699, during a time of persecution of Sikhs and Hindus, Guru Gobind Singh founded the Khalsa, a brotherhood of committed Sikhs who would uphold the Sikh faith as well as fight when necessary against persecution.

Becoming a member of the Khalsa is a voluntary step, involving a more disciplined way of life, both spiritually and physically. Initiation into the Khalsa usually takes place at the festival of **Baisakhi** but it can be at any time. Five members of the Khalsa perform the ceremony, at which a special sweet liquid, **amrit**, is drunk and sprinkled on the candidates, and they are reminded of the duties and responsibilities of Khalsa Sikhs.

Members of the Khalsa are required to wear the five Ks – symbols that mark them out as Sikhs. Other Sikhs are encouraged to wear them as well. The five Ks are as follows:

- The **kanga**: this is the comb which keeps the hair tidy and is a symbol of discipline.
- The **kara**: a bangle; a symbol of one God, one brotherhood, and that truth is eternal. Now made of steel to symbolise strength.
- The **kacchera**: these are long, above-the-knee, breeches, worn to show that a Sikh was always ready to ride to battle in defence of just causes. The dhoti, the garb worn at the time of Guru Gobind Singh, was not suitable for horseback riding.
- The **kirpan**; a sword, similarly a sign of the Sikh's willingness to fight injustice, protect the vulnerable and defend religious freedom including that of non-Sikhs. British Sikhs usually carry or wear a miniature kirpan.
- The **kesh**: long uncut hair (which in Indian tradition is a sign of wisdom), which must be kept very neat. The turban is not one of the five Ks, but is worn to keep the hair tidy. It is not worn by primary school age children and boys' long hair is gathered together and tied up in a handkerchief on the top of their heads. The long hair rule is not observed rigorously by all Sikhs in Britain.

The Guru Granth Sahib teaches belief in one God and in reincarnation. Narcotics are forbidden. Many hymns praise the beauty of the natural world, and although animals may be eaten they must not be abused in the process of slaughter.

Main festivals

- **Gurpurb** – Festivals commemorating events in the lives of the Gurus. One of the best known is Guru Nanak's birthday.
- **Baisakhi**, the foundation of the Khalsa, is celebrated in April. Themes are commitment, discipline, religious freedom, equality.
- At **Hola Mohalla**, while Hindus celebrate with games and pranks Sikhs have contests of horsemanship, wrestling, etc. for both men and women, developing the idea of Sikh readiness to fight for just causes.

Places of pilgrimage

Amritsar in the Punjab, India-site of the Golden Temple.

Artefacts

Comb (kanga), bangle (kara) and breeches (kacchera), plus sword brooch.

Bibliography

References

Books and articles

Anthony, S (1940) *The child's discovery of death.* London: Kegan Paul, Trench Trubner and Co.

Bastide, D (1992) *Good practice in primary religious education 4–11*, 9th edn. Abingdon: Falmer.

Baumfield, V (2002) *Thinking through religious education.* Cambridge: Chris Kingston Publishing.

Bloom, BS. (ed.) *Taxonomy of educational objectives: the classification of educational goals.* Philadelphia, PA: Susan Fauer Company. pp201–7.

Cairney,T (1990) *Teaching reading comprehension.* Oxford: Oxford University Press.

Coles, R (1990) *The spiritual life of children.* London: HarperCollins.

Cooling, T (2000) Theology as the basis for religious education, in Grimmitt, MH (ed.), *Pedagogies of religious education: case studies in the research and development of good pedagogic practice in RE.* Great Wakering: McCrimmons Publishing Co.

Daniels, H (ed.) (2005) *An introduction to Vygotsky*, 2nd edn. Abingdon: Routledge.

Dawkins, R (2006) *The God delusion.* London: Bantam Press.

Donaldson, M (1978) *Children's minds.* London: Fontana Press.

Eliot, TS (1955) *The four quartets.* London: Faber and Faber.

Fisher, R (1990) *Teaching children to think.* Oxford: Blackwell.

Fowler, J ([1981] 1995) *Stages of faith.* San Francisco, CA: HarperCollins.

Gilligan, C (1982) *In a different voice.* Cambridge, MA: University of Harvard Press.

Gobbles Rand, G (1986) *The Bible: a children's playground.* London: SCM.

Goldman, RJ (1964) *Religious thinking from childhood to adolescence.* Abingdon: Routledge & Kegan Paul.

Grimmitt, MH et al. (1991) *A gift to the child.* Hemel Hempstead: Simon & Schuster Education.

Grimmitt, MH (ed.) (2000) *Pedagogies of religious education: case studies in the research and development of good pedagogic practice in RE.* Great Wakering: McCrimmons Publishing Co.

Grimmitt, MH et al. (2006) *A gift to the child 2.* Bury: Articles of Faith.

Hammond, J et al. (1990) *New Methods in RE teaching: An experiential approach.* Harlow: Oliver and Boyd.

Heller, D (1986) *The children's God.* Chicago, IL: University of Chicago.

Hollindale, P. (1992) *Ideology and the children's book.* Stroud: Thimble Press.

Holm, A (1989) *I am David.* London: World Mammoth.

Hughes, S (1977) *Dogger.* London: Bodley Head.

Hull, J (1991) *God–talk with young children.* Birmingham: Christian Education Movement.

Inkpen, M (1995) *Nothing.* London: Hodder Children's Books.

Kohlberg, L et al. (1987) *Child psychology and childhood education: a cognitive–developmental view.* Harlow: Longman.

Lipman, M (1991) *Thinking in education.* Cambridge: Cambridge University Press.

Loukes, M (1965) *Teenage religion.* London: SCM.

McCreery, E (2000) Promoting children's spiritual development: a review of the literature and an investigation into the attitudes of teachers. Unpublished Ph.D. dissertation, University of Surrey,

Roehampton.

Nagy, M (1959) The child's view of death, in Feifel, H (ed.) *The meaning of death*. New York: McGraw-Hill.

Phillips, S (2003) *Making RE make sense: Theatre of Learning, experimental RE*. Bristol: Standards in Education.

Piaget, J (1968) *Judgment and reasoning in the child*. Totowa, NJ: Littlefield, Adams, & Co.

Postman, N (1985) *Teaching as a subversive activity*. London: Random House.

Rizzuto, AM (1979) *The birth of the living god: a psychoanalytic study*. Chicago, IL: University of Chicago Press.

Toledo Guiding Principles on Teaching about Religions and Beliefs in Public Schools (2007) Office for Democratic Institutions and Human Rights www.firstamendmentcenter.org/pdf/Toledo_Guiding_-Principles.pdf (accessed January 2008).

Government documentation

1944 Education Act

1988 Education Reform Act

DfE (1994) *Circular 1/94: Religious education and collective worship*. London: Department for Education. 31 January.

DfEE (1999) *All our futures: Creativity, culture and education*. Report of the National Advisory Committee on Creative and Cultural Education.

DfES (2003) *Excellence and Enjoyment* (The Robinson Report). London: Department for Education and Skills.

DfES (2007) *Diversity and citizenship: Curriculum review*. Nottingham: Department for Education and Skills. (Ref. 00045–2007DOM–EN.)

DFID, DfES, QCA, DEA, British Council (2005) *Developing the global dimension in the school curriculum*. London: DFID. (DfES reference: 1409–2005DOC–EN.)

Ofsted (2007) *Making sense of religion*. London: Ofsted. (HMI No. 070045.)

QCA (2004) *Religious education: the Non–Statutory National Framework*. London: Qualifications and Curriculum Authority/DfES.

SCAA (1994) *Model syllabuses*. London: School Curriculum and Assessment Authority.

SCAA (1995) *Spiritual and moral development*. SCAA Discussion Paper No. 3. London: SCAA.

DVD/video

Monkey King and other tales. Manchester: Clear Vision Trust.

Testament: The Bible in animation. London: BBC2.

Water, Moon, Candle, Tree and Sword. Wetherby: Channel 4 Learning.

Recommended reading

These are just a sample of the many children's books available, grouped by theme:

Children's picture books

Picture books with the theme of friendship

Allen, P (1992) *Black dog*. Hawthorn, Victoria: Penguin Puffin Australia.

Fox, M (1984) *William Gordon Macdonald Partridge*. New South Wales: Scholastic Australia.

Jeffers, O (2005) *Lost and found*. London: HarperCollins.

Picture books with the theme of identity

Cooke, T (1996) *So much.* London: Walker Books.

Hoffman, M (1997) *An angel just like me.* London: Frances Lincoln.

Inkpen, M (1995) *Nothing.* London: Hodder Children's Books.

Picture books on change, loss, bereavement

Browne, A (1990) *Changes.* London: Walker Books.

Hughes, S (1977) *Dogger.* London: Bodley Head. (This story also exemplifies kindness without being overly didactic.)

Varley, S (1984) *Badger's parting gifts.* London: Anderson Press.

Viorst, J (1972) *The tenth good thing about Barney.* London: Collins.

Wilhem, H (1985) *I'll always love you.* New York: Dragonfly.

Picture books on family relationships and reconciliation

Browne, A (1983) *Gorilla.* London: Julia MacRae.

Hoban, R (1969) *A baby sister for Frances.* London: Faber and Faber.

Sendak, M (1967) *Where the wild things are.* London: Bodley Head.

Wells, R (1977) *Morris's disappearing bag: a Christmas story.* London: Kestrel Books.

Picture books with illustrations that can evoke awe and wonder

Anno, M (1985) *Anno's counting book.* London: Macmillan Children's.

Briggs, R (1978) *The snowman.* London: Hamish Hamilton.

Jeffers, O (2004) *How to catch a star.* London: HarperCollins.

Kitamura, S (1989) *UFO diary.* London: Red Fox.

Children's novels

Burnett, F (1951) *The secret garden.* London: Penguin Books. (A story about the redemptive power of nature.)

King–Smith D (1989) *Martin's mice.* London: Puffin. (Much of Dick King–Smith's work for older children deals with the development of identity and family relationships.)

Naidoo, B (2001) *The other side of truth.* London: HarperCollins. (A book about refugees exploring issues of exile and freedom.)

Magorian, M (1983) *Goodnight, Mister Tom.* London: Puffin. (Set during the Second World War this brave book deals with child abuse as well as loss and love.)

White, EB (1963) *Charlotte's web.* London: Penguin. (A classic story on bereavement and loss.)

Wilson, J (2000) *Vicky Angel.* London: Doubleday. (A story on bereavement but also on the problematic side of friendship.)

Some explicitly religious stories

Bible stories

Allan, N (1993) *Jesus' Christmas party.* London: Red Fox.

Bruna, D (1976) *The Christmas story.* London: Methuen.

Pieńkowski, J (1984) *Christmas: the King James Version,* with pictures by Jan Pienkowski. London: Heinemann. (A version of the Christmas story for older children. The silhouette illustrations bring out the darker side. It is an introduction to the poetic language of the King James Version.)

Ray, J (1997) *In the beginning: Bible stories.* London: Orchard.

Spier, J (1986) *The Book of Jonah.* London: Hodder.

Wildsmith, B (1993) *The Easter story.* Oxford: Oxford University Press.

Stories from other principal religions in the United Kingdom

Geras, A (1990) *My grandmother's stories: a collection of Jewish folk tales.* London: Heinemann.

Khan, N (1999) *Twenty Jataka tales retold.* Rochester, VT: Inner Traditions.

Ramachandran, A (1979) *The story of Hanuman.* London: A & C Black.

Souhami, J (1997) *Rama and the demon king: an ancient tale from India.* London: Frances Lincoln.

Palmer, S and Breuilly, E (1993) *A tapestry of tales.* London: Collins Educational. (An anthology of religious stories written with the pimary RE teacher in mind. These include stories from the Ancient World, native peoples as well as the major religions.)

Many children's stories on religions are most easily available on line. We would particularly recommend.

www.buddhanet.net

www.sikhnet.com

The Evans publishing house also has excellent series of non–fiction and stories from religion series: www.evansbooks.co.uk.

Other helpful resources grouped by topic/ subject area

The principles and practice of RE

Bastide, D (ed.) (1992) *Good practice in primary religious education 4–11.* Abingdon: Falmer.

Bastide, D (2004) *Religious education 4–11*, 2nd edn. Abingdon: Routledge.

Hoodless, P, Bermingham, S, McCreery, E and Bowen, P (2003) *Teaching humanities in primary schools.* Exeter: Learning Matters.

Langtree, G (1997) *Are you ready? Developing quality religious education in primary schools.* Norwich: R.M.E.P.

Specific research and approaches in the teaching of RE

Grimmitt, MH (ed.) (2000) *Pedagogies of religious education: case studies in the research and development of good pedagogic practice in RE.* Great Wakering: McCrimmons.

Grimmitt, MH et al. (1991) *A gift to the child.* Hemel Hempstead: Simon & Schuster Education.

Grimmitt, MH et al. (2006) *A gift to the child 2.* Bury: Articles of Faith. (The 'Gift to the Child' Pack of resources. This includes lesson scripts supported by materials.)

Jackson, R (1997) *Religious education: an interpretive approach.* London: Hodder & Stoughton.

Watson, B and Thompson, P (2007) *The effective teaching of religious education.* Harlow: Pearson Longman.

Child development

Fowler, J (1995) *Stages of faith.* San Francisco, CA: HarperCollins.

Wood, D (1998) *How children think and learn*, 2nd edn. Oxford: Blackwell.

Children and bereavement

Leaman, O (1995) *Death and loss: compassionate approaches in the classroom*. London: Cassell.
Mallon, B (1998) *Helping children manage loss*. London: Jessica Kingsley.

Thinking skills

Fisher, R (1990) *Teaching children to think*. Oxford: Blackwell.
Higgins, S with Baumfield, V (2003) *Thinking through primary teaching*. Cambridge: Chris Kingston Publishing.

Spirituality and RE

Best, R (ed.) (1996) *Education, spirituality and the whole child*. London: Cassell.
Erricker, C et al. (1997) *The education of the whole child*. London: Cassell.
Erricker, C et al. (ed.) (2001) *Spiritual education: religious cultural and social differences*. Brighton: Academic Press
Myers, B (1997) *Young children and spirituality*. Abingdon: Routledge.

Ethnographic issues and RE

McCreery, E, Jones, L and Holmes, R (2007) Why do Muslim parents want Muslim schools?, *Early Years*, 27 (3): 203–20.
Nesbitt, E (2004) *Intercultural education: ethnographic and religious approaches*. Brighton: Academic Press.

Global citizenship

Burns, S and Lamont, G (1998) *Values and visions: DEP*. London: Hodder & Stoughton.
Young, M (2002) *Global citizenship. The handbook for primary teaching*. Cambridge: Oxfam and Chris Kingston Publishing.

ICT and RE

Hughes, S (2002) *ICT in RE*. Harlow: Pearson.

Using drama in the primary classroom

Fleming, M (2001) *Teaching drama in primary and secondary schools*. London: David Fulton.
Heathcote, D and Bolton, G (1995) *Drama for learning: Dorothy Heathcote's mantle of the expert approach to education*. Portsmouth, NH: Heinemann.

Journals

British Journal of Religious Education (BJRE) (Taylor and Francis)
International Journal of Spiritual Education (Taylor and Francis)
Journal of Beliefs and Values (Taylor and Francis)

Useful websites

www.reonline.org.uk. This is your springboard to a multitude of resources and links for RE.
www.arcworld.org. A window into the world of religion and conservation.
www.articlesoffaith.co.uk. A company that sells religious artefacts for use in educational settings

www.bbc.co.uk/religion. This website will inform you about programmes about religion and also has very useful introduction to religions and further reading on them.

www.dialogueworks.co.uk. A website on the use of the community of enquiry.

www.hospicenet.org. A helpful outline of children's understanding of death and experience of bereavement.

www.osdemethodology.org.uk. A website promoting social justice through education.

www.retoday.org.uk. This website offers a catalogue for lots of materials supporting RE. Also available from the website is RE Today, an attractive periodical offering accessible guidance, ideas and practical examples for teaching RE at all levels.

www.sapere.net. Philosophy for children.

Multimedia resources

reonline reviews commercially produce multimedia resources. We especially recommend:

Water, Moon, Candle, Tree and Sword. Wetherby (Channel 4Learning). (Testament stories from five faiths are linked to children of the faith.)

Eggshells and Thunderbolts available from the Culham Institute at www.culham.ac.uk. (This is a training pack showing examples of RE lessons across the key stages.)

Added to the page reference 'f' denotes a figure.